A note to teachers and parents

This new edition of the Key Stage 2 Maths Revision Guide is fully aligned to the National Numeracy Strategy Framework. The increased emphasis on **number work and calculations**, with both written and mental calculation strategies included, is complemented by the use **of reduced line lengths, simple language, diagrams and colour** to further enhance the clarity of explanations. We believe that success in maths comes from understanding the underlying principles behind the subject and not from a collection of numerous 'simple steps' learnt by rote.

This book was produced and revised to meet with specific criteria…

- To produce excellent revision notes for the end of Key Stage 2 National Curriculum Tests (SATs) for levels 3–5 inclusive and to ensure that everything in the Programme of Study for this Key Stage has been covered – **and nothing more**.
- To encourage and retain the interest of a child at Key Stage 2.
- To cover the material without reference to specific levels. Every page is accessible to all pupils, but obviously some will absorb and understand more than others. All pupils should be encouraged to cover as much as possible of every topic.
- To help teachers and parents by giving them a concise summary of the work that is covered throughout school years 3–6.
- To provide appropriate practice questions on each page to ensure that work has been understood. Further practice is provided in the accompanying Pupil Worksheets.

A note about the consultant editor

This book has been fully revised under the expert guidance of Elaine Foster, National Numeracy Strategy Consultant and Advisory Teacher. In addition to over 20 years teaching experience, Elaine was involved in writing and developing the Primary Mathematics Scheme for a local authority, and trains teachers in acclaimed interactive teaching methods.

A note to the pupil

We're sure that you will enjoy using this book, but to make the most of it…

- Read each section carefully and then answer the questions set. Have your answers checked regularly and go back through any work that you have got wrong.
- Try to get into a routine. Work through the book steadily, don't rush and don't try to do too much at once.

Good Luck!

Contents

Numbers

4 The Value of Numbers, The Value of Zero

5 Reading and Writing Numbers

6 Ordering Numbers, Ordering Decimals

7 Negative Numbers, Less Than or Greater Than

8 Multiplying by 10 and 100, Dividing by 10 and 100

9 Multiplying and Dividing by 1000, Multiplying and Dividing Decimals by 10 and 100

10 Calculating, Adding and Subtracting – The Basic Skills

11 Adding and Subtracting – By Other Means

12 Adding and Subtracting – Written Methods, Adding and Subtracting Decimals

13 Multiplying and Dividing – Basic Skills

14 Multiplying and Dividing – Some Useful Methods

15 Multiplying – Written Methods

16 Dividing – Written Methods

17 Multiplying and Dividing Decimals

18 Dividing – Remainders

19 Calculations – Negative Numbers

20 Multiples, Lowest Common Multiple, Factors

21 Square Numbers, Prime Numbers, Prime Factors

22 Number Patterns

23 Formulas

24 Fractions

25 Simplifying Fractions, Mixed Numbers, Comparing Fractions

26 Percentages, Number Lines

27 Finding a Fraction of an Amount, Finding a Percentage of an Amount

28 Proportions and Ratios, Percentage of the Rest

29 Solving Problems

30 Estimating, Rounding

31 Co-ordinates

Contents

Handling Data

50 Collecting Data

51 Bar Charts, Pictograms

52 Pie Charts, Sorting Diagrams

53 Line Graphs, Types of Data

54 Averages, The Range

55 Probability, Predicting Outcomes

Shape, Space and Measures

32 Describing Shapes, Polygons

33 Triangles, Quadrilaterals, Diagonals of a Quadrilateral

34 3-Dimensional Shapes, Polyhedrons, Prisms

35 Angles, Types of Angle

36 Measuring Angles, Drawing Angles

37 Calculating Angles

38 Line Symmetry, Reflection

39 Translation, Rotation

40 Congruent Shapes, Tessellations

41 Making 3-D Models

42 Length

43 Mass

44 Capacity

45 Time, Finding the Difference in Time, The 24 Hour Clock

46 Imperial Units, Length, Mass, Capacity, Estimating Measures

47 Perimeter

48 Area

49 More Area

56 **Index**

Numbers

The Value of Numbers

Numbers are made up of **digits**, and the position of each digit tells us its value. This is called the **place value** of the digit.

1 Write down the value of the underlined digit in each of the numbers below:
- **a)** 7<u>4</u>9
- **b)** 25<u>3</u>8
- **c)** 34<u>3</u>
- **d)** <u>7</u>642
- **e)** 39<u>5</u>4
- **f)** <u>4</u>061
- **g)** 910<u>0</u>

2 Split these numbers up into thousands, hundreds, tens and units:
- **a)** 2115
- **b)** 1473
- **c)** 2063
- **d)** 8100
- **e)** 9040
- **f)** 4001

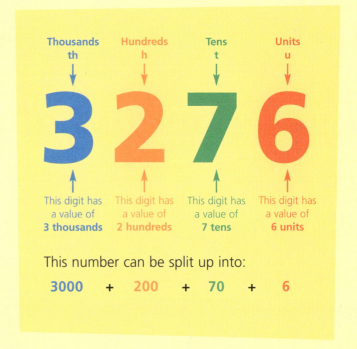

This number can be split up into:

3000 + **200** + **70** + **6**

A **decimal point** is used when numbers are not whole, to show where the part of the number that is less than 1 starts. The part of the number after the decimal point is a **decimal fraction**.

3 Write down the value of the underlined digit in each of the numbers below:
- **a)** 2.3<u>6</u>
- **b)** 32.<u>7</u>4
- **c)** 18.25<u>3</u>
- **d)** 1.0<u>1</u>5
- **e)** 2.<u>3</u>01
- **f)** 8.00<u>3</u>

4 Split these numbers up into tens, units, tenths, hundredths and thousandths.
- **a)** 63.456
- **b)** 8.8
- **c)** 5.003
- **d)** 9.786
- **e)** 12.12
- **f)** 10.352

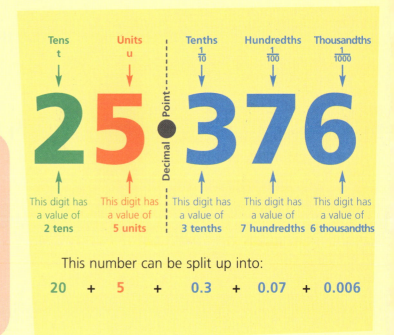

This number can be split up into:

20 + **5** + **0.3** + **0.07** + **0.006**

The Value of Zero

Zeros in numbers are **very important**. They keep the rest of the digits in their place. Just imagine 304 without its zero, it would only be 34! And 602.08 would only be 62.8. Zeros that don't help to keep other digits in their places aren't needed. So 0034 can be written as 34, and 00305.4600 can be written as 305.46.

5 Decide which zeros are not needed and rewrite the numbers without them.
- **a)** 056
- **b)** 00908
- **c)** 36.500
- **d)** 040.30
- **e)** 0701.0200
- **f)** 00300.600

Reading and Writing Numbers

Numbers can be written in **words** and **digits** (or figures). You can use the place value of each digit to help you write a number…

… in WORDS

th   h   t   u

2143

is written:
Two thousand, one hundred and forty three

… and FIGURES

One thousand and seven is written:

th   h   t   u

1007

↑   ↑
Extra zeros to keep the 1 and 7 in their place.

The digits of very big numbers can be grouped into millions, thousands and hundreds. Always start at the right of the number and work to the left, grouping the digits in threes:

millions   thousands

12 360 714

is written:
Twelve million, three hundred and sixty thousand, seven hundred and fourteen.

It is a good idea to have small gaps between each group of three figures. Doing this makes very big numbers easier to read.

Four million, fifteen thousand and thirty is written:

4 015 030

↑   ↑
Small gaps

---

6 Write these numbers in words:
a) 75   b) 309   c) 6014

7 Write these numbers in figures:
a) Four hundred and eleven
b) Eight thousand and twenty
c) Eleven thousand and eleven

8 Write these numbers in figures:
a) Three hundred and five thousand, one hundred and seven
b) Twelve million and fifty thousand

9 Write these numbers in words:
a) 407 111   b) 35 604 760   c) 10 010 001

Numbers

Ordering Numbers

Numbers often need to be placed in order of size, from the smallest to the largest or the largest to the smallest. You can use a **number line** to help you decide the correct order of the numbers. You also need to compare the values of the digits, working from left to right. Here is part of a number line:

A number line is a very special line. It is as long as you can possibly imagine and goes up in tiny little steps.

If we have the numbers **320** and **318**, the first digit in both numbers has the same value, but the second digit in **320** has a value of **2** tens which is bigger than the **1** ten in **318**. The value of the third digit in both numbers now doesn't matter and so **320** is bigger than **318**.

Ordering Decimals

When you put numbers with decimals in order, the method is just the same. Simply use the number line to help you decide the correct order of the numbers. Remember to compare the values of the digits on the left first and then work to the right.

You should read or say 7.25 as 'seven point two five'.

If we have the decimals **7.3** and **7.25** the first digit in both decimals has the same value but the second digit in **7.3** has a value of **3** tenths which is bigger than the **2** tenths in **7.25** and so **7.3** is bigger than **7.25**.

10 Which is bigger?
a) 3739 or 3753 b) 2014 or 2103

11 On the planet Thrang the Mega Millions lottery winning balls were: **513, 369, 1037, 402, 521** and **1101**. Put these balls in order starting with the smallest.

12 Which number is the smallest?
a) 2.35 or 2.17   b) 13.163 or 13.2

13 Put these numbers in order, starting with the smallest:
a) 23.56, 22.71, 22.8, 23.2
b) 126.4, 126.08, 125.97, 126.36
c) 7.183, 7.21, 7.191, 7.3

14 Give the number which is halfway between 12.5 and 12.6.

Negative Numbers

The scale on a thermometer is also a **number line**. Thermometers that are used to measure the temperature on very cold days need numbers that are **less than 0**. These are called **negative numbers**.

The temperature on this thermometer is **-2°C**.

Negative numbers are placed on the number line to the left of 0. The further to the **right** that a number is on the number line, the **bigger** it is. The **smaller** the number is, the further **left** it is on the number line.

-8 is less than -4 or
-4 is greater than -8
-2 is less than 1 or
1 is greater than -2

15 Write down the temperature on these thermometers:

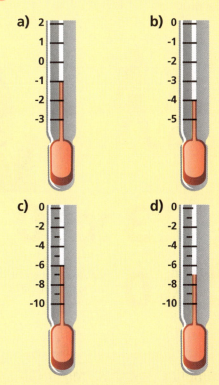

Which temperature is the coldest?

16 **a)** Make a copy of the number line below, and place these numbers on it.

-3.5   2.5   -1.5   -6.5

b) Write these numbers down in order, starting with the smallest:

1   -4   3.5   -2.5   -7   0

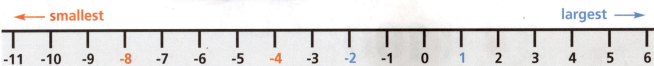

← **smallest**   **largest** →

-11 -10 -9 -8 -7 -6 -5 -4 -3 -2 -1 0 1 2 3 4 5 6

Less Than or Greater Than

There are some special symbols which can be used to save having to write 'less than' or 'greater than'.

17 Which of these statements are correct?
a) 8 > 3   **b)** 27 < 24.2   **c)** 3.6 > 5

18 Write these pairs of numbers with the correct symbol in between:
a) 9, 4   **b)** 13, 12.5   **c)** 21, 20.6

The arrow of these symbols always points to the smallest number.

2 is less than 3 can be written as: **2 < 3**

-4 is greater than -5 can be written as: **-4 > -5**

Numbers

Multiplying by 10 and 100

If you **multiply** a number by **10**, the digits all move **one place** to the **left**.

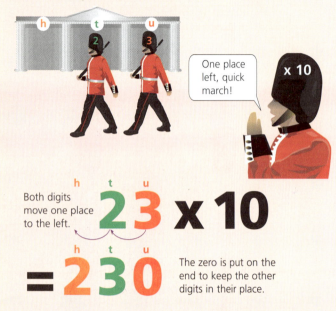

One place left, quick march!

x 10

Both digits move one place to the left.

23 x 10

= 230

The zero is put on the end to keep the other digits in their place.

If you **multiply** a number by **100**, the digits all move **two places** to the **left**.

Two places left, quick march!

x 100

Two places to the left.

34 x 100

= 3400

Two zeros put on the end.

Dividing by 10 and 100

Dividing is the **opposite** of **multiplying** so it has the opposite effect. If you **divide** a number by **10** the digits all move **one place** to the **right**.

One place right, quick march!

÷ 10

One place to the right.

360 ÷ 10

= 36

The zero is no longer needed.

If you **divide** a number by **100**, the digits all move **two places** to the **right**.

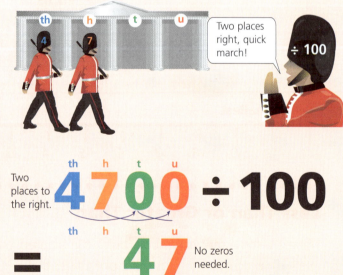

Two places right, quick march!

÷ 100

Two places to the right.

4700 ÷ 100

= 47

No zeros needed.

---

19 Work out:
a) 35 x 10   b) 57 x 10   c) 248 x 10
d) 307 x 10   e) 260 x 10   f) 510 x 10

20 What is:
a) 28 x 100   b) 64 x 100   c) 157 x 100
d) 205 x 100   e) 30 x 100   f) 300 x 100

21 Calculate:
a) 340 ÷ 10   b) 2360 ÷ 10
c) 5700 ÷ 10   d) 8300 ÷ 100
e) 96 000 ÷ 100   f) 104 000 ÷ 100

Multiplying and Dividing by 1000

When you **multiply** or **divide** by **1000**, the digits move **three places** along. Three to the **LEFT** when **multiplying**. Three to the **RIGHT** when **dividing**.

Examples:

36	x	1000	=	36 000
510	x	1000	=	510 000
27 000	÷	1000	=	27
420 000	÷	1000	=	420

 See if you can do these:
a) 12 x 1000   b) 351 x 1000
c) 920 x 1000   d) 5 x 1000

23 See if you can do these:
a) 75 000 ÷ 1000   b) 254 000 ÷ 1000
c) 270 000 ÷ 1000   d) 1000 ÷ 1000

Multiplying and Dividing Decimals by 10 and 100

You can multiply and divide **decimals** in just the same way. The decimal point **must not move**. The digits move to the **left** when **multiplying** and to the **right** when **dividing**. **One** place for **10** and **two** places for **100**.

Some further examples:

32.6	x	10	=	326
0.274	x	100	=	27.4
42.8	÷	10	=	4.28
24.5	÷	100	=	0.245

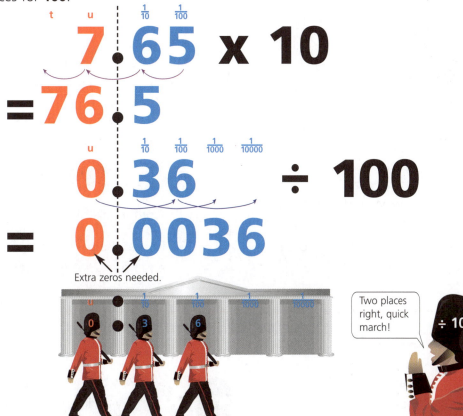

Extra zeros needed.

Two places right, quick march!

÷ 100

24 Try these for yourself:
a) 24.2 x 10   b) 3.214 x 100   c) 3.75 x 100   d) 7.8 x 100   e) 0.015 x 100   f) 1.305 x 100
g) 3.96 ÷ 10   h) 281.3 ÷ 10   i) 3.65 ÷ 100   j) 4.1 ÷ 100   k) 20 ÷ 100   l) 3261.45 ÷ 100

Numbers

Calculating

You need to be able to **add** (+), **subtract** (–), **multiply** (x) and **divide** (÷) numbers. When faced with any calculation you should ask yourself:

1 Can I do it in my head? If the answer is **no**, ask yourself…

2 Can I do it if I write it down? If the answer is still **no**, you could…

3 Use a calculator, but only if you are allowed to.

There are many different ways of doing the same calculation. It is well worth practising a few, but in the end choose the method you are most comfortable with.

Adding and Subtracting – The Basic Skills

You need to be able to **add** or **subtract** any two numbers **up to 20** in your head. You should try to do this without counting on your fingers. The key to success is **regular practice**… anywhere and at anytime.

5 + 6 = 11
7 + 8 = 15
9 + 10 = 19

Try these exercises – in your head, or say them out loud.

1 1 + 2 = , 3 + 4 = , 5 + 6 = , 7 + 8 = , 9 + 10 = , 11 + 12 = , 13 + 14 = , 15 + 16 = , 17 + 18 = , 19 + 20 = … and now do them backwards.

2 20 – 1 = , 19 – 2 = , 18 – 3 = , 17 – 4 = , 16 – 5 = , 15 – 6 = , 14 – 7 = , 13 – 8 = , 12 – 9 = , 11 – 10 = .

3 1 + 2 + 3 = , 2 + 3 + 4 = , 3 + 4 + 5 = 4 + 5 + 6 = , 5 + 6 + 7 = .

4 17 – 3 = 14, how many other pairs of numbers between 1 and 20 have a difference of 14?

5 Find all the pairs of two-digit numbers that add up to 29. Repeat for other numbers.

Some Useful Tips

Make your own exercises up

Every time you go shopping try adding up the prices

Test a grown up and see if you can beat them

Have a game of darts and work out the total score of three darts.

Adding and Subtracting
– By Other Means

1

Use near doubles...
if the numbers are nearly the same.
e.g. 75 + 78
is double 75 add 3 = 150 + 3 = 153
e.g. 115 + 87
is double 100 add 15 and
take away 13 = 202

2

Count on or back
e.g. 143 + 20
can be found by doing
143 + 10 + 10 = 163
e.g. 917 – 300
can be found by doing
917 – 100 – 100 – 100 = 617

3

Split the numbers up
e.g. 34 + 57
= 30 + 4 + 50 + 7
= 80 + 11
= 91

4

Use 'nearly numbers'
e.g. 45 – 29 is nearly 45 – 30
45 – 30 = 15
and so 45 – 29
= 15 + 1 = 16

5

Use a blank number line
You can use a number line to help you
with all of these methods
e.g. 45 – 29 = 16

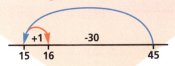

25 Use whichever method you choose to answer these:
a) 28 + 54   b) 423 – 48   c) 85 + 87   d) 129 + 219
e) 388 + 413   f) 573 – 81   g) 40 + 50 + 60 + 70   h) 4.8 + 2.4
i) 84 + 75   j) 6000 – 2155   k) 6.2 – 3.9   l) 13.1 – 7.5
m) 36 + 14 + 27   n) 61 + 65 + 67   o) 2.13 + 3.4   p) 4.9 – 3.2

Checking Your Answer

Since adding and subtracting are **opposites**, you
can use this to **check your answer**.

26 Use an opposite to check your answers
to Question 25.

23 + 18 = 41
and so...

41 – 18 = 23
or
41 – 23 = 18

If you have done an **addition**,
check it with **subtraction**

25 – 9 = 16
and so...

16 + 9 = 25

If you have done a **subtraction**,
check it with **addition**

Numbers

Adding and Subtracting – Written Methods

As the numbers you are adding or subtracting get bigger and bigger, you will need to set them out with one number above the other. Space the digits out so that you have room to work, and keep them in nice, **neat columns**.

5643 + 874 is set out:

Work from right to left.

Add the units first
3 + 4 = 7

4 + 7 = 11
so put 1 down and carry 1 into the hundreds column.

6 + 8 + the 1 that was carried is 15. Put 5 down and carry 1.

5 + 1 = 6

4428 – 765 is set out:

Work from right to left.

Start with the units again. 8 – 5 = 3

2 – 6 can't be done, so 1 is borrowed from the hundreds column, leaving 3 behind. 1 hundred = 10 tens so we now have 10 + 2 = 12 tens. 12 – 6 = 6.

3 – 7 can't be done, so 10 hundreds are borrowed from the thousands column. 13 – 7 = 6

We are left with 3 – nothing which is 3.

Adding and Subtracting Decimals

Decimals are **added** and **subtracted** in just the same way. When the numbers are written down with one above the other, the **decimal points** must be kept in a nice, **neat column**.

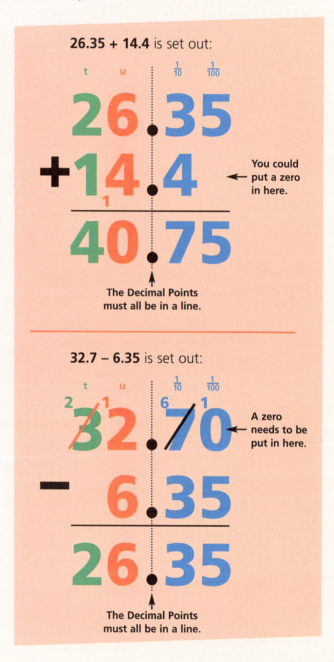

26.35 + 14.4 is set out:

You could put a zero in here.

The Decimal Points must all be in a line.

32.7 – 6.35 is set out:

A zero needs to be put in here.

The Decimal Points must all be in a line.

---

27 Set these out carefully and find the answers:

a) 365 + 58   **b)** 429 + 732

c) 4364 + 865   **d)** 695 – 188

e) 729 – 354   **f)** 3451 – 1693

28 Set these out carefully and find the answers:

a) 12.6 + 3.7   **b)** 24.51 + 14.87

c) 183.28 + 51.34   **d)** 96.2 + 13.73

e) 245.76 + 82.8   **f)** 211.23 + 12.09

29 **a)** 23.2 – 16.4   **b)** 8.76 – 5.69

c) 162.91 – 78.45   **d)** 84.1 – 3.29

e) 162.36 – 54.8   **f)** 291.22 – 79.3

Multiplying and Dividing
– Basic Skills

Multiplying and dividing are **opposites**. Being able to do one helps you with the other. If you want to be good at it you must know your **times tables**. You need to know everything from 1 x 1 up to 10 x 10.

If you have difficulty with your times tables, learn them one at a time. Start with the easier ones such as 1, 2, 5 and 10. Then do the harder ones. The key to success with this is **regular practice**.

X	1	2	3	4	5	6	7	8	9	10
1	1	2	3	4	5	6	7	8	9	10
2	2	4	6	8	10	12	14	16	18	20
3	3	6	9	12	15	18	21	24	27	30
4	4	8	12	16	20	24	28	32	36	40
5	5	10	15	20	25	30	35	40	45	50
6	6	12	18	24	30	36	42	48	54	60
7	7	14	21	28	35	42	49	56	63	70
8	8	16	24	32	40	48	56	64	72	80
9	9	18	27	36	45	54	63	72	81	90
10	10	20	30	40	50	60	70	80	90	100

Some Useful Tips

Try chanting out 1 x 4 = 4, 2 x 4 = 8, 3 x 4 = 12 and so on.

Make your own copy of the grid and stick it on a wall where you can see it easily.

Make it into a song.

Say them forwards then say them backwards.

Work with a friend, say them together, take it in turns to test each other.

6 x 8 = 8 x 6. Use patterns to help.

Take every opportunity to practise.

Numbers

Multiplying and Dividing – Some Useful Methods

1. Doubling

Doubling numbers can be used to help you multiply all sorts of bigger numbers. All you have to remember is if you want to multiply a number…

…**by 2** – you double it

…**by 4** – you double it and double it again

…**by 8** – you double it, double it again and double it again

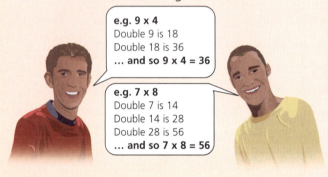

e.g. 9 x 4
Double 9 is 18
Double 18 is 36
… and so 9 x 4 = 36

e.g. 7 x 8
Double 7 is 14
Double 14 is 28
Double 28 is 56
… and so 7 x 8 = 56

30 Try using doubling to do these:
a) 7 x 4   **b)** 7 x 8   **c)** 15 x 8   **d)** 12 x 16

2. Halving

Halving numbers can be used to help you divide by all sorts of bigger numbers. It's the opposite process to doubling. All you have to remember is if you want to divide a number...

…**by 2** – you halve it

…**by 4** – you halve it and halve it again

…**by 8** – you halve it, halve it again and halve it again

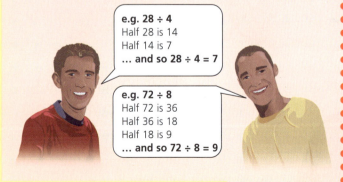

e.g. 28 ÷ 4
Half 28 is 14
Half 14 is 7
… and so 28 ÷ 4 = 7

e.g. 72 ÷ 8
Half 72 is 36
Half 36 is 18
Half 18 is 9
… and so 72 ÷ 8 = 9

31 Try these:
a) 64 ÷ 8   **b)** 100 ÷ 4   **c)** 136 ÷ 8

3. Splitting your Numbers Up Into Multiples of 10 and Units

Splitting your numbers up into multiples of 10 and units can also be used. Remember that brackets show the order in which the calculations must be done.

e.g. 15 x 12
= (15 x 10) + (15 x 2)
= 150 + 30
= 180

e.g. 9 x 8
= (9 x 10) − (9 x 2)
= 90 − 18
= 72

e.g. 11 x 25
= (11 x 20) + (11 x 5)
= 220 + 55
= 275

e.g. 11 x 25
= (11 x 30) − (11 x 5)
= 330 − 55
= 275

e.g. 14 x 19
= (14 x 20) − (14 x 1)
= 280 − 14
= 266

32 Use whichever method you find easiest for each of these:
a) 14 x 15   **b)** 39 x 25   **c)** 17 x 12
d) 24 x 16   **e)** 41 x 15   **f)** 18 x 22

Multiplying – Written Methods

Whichever method you choose always start by getting a rough estimate of the answer first. You should use this estimate to check your answer.

To work out **246 x 9**:
246 x 9 is roughly **200 x 10 = 2000.**

If your answer is not between 1500 and 2500, check your working out.

An easy way to work it out is to multiply the value of each digit of 246 by 9

$$200 \times 9 = 1800$$
$$40 \times 9 = 360$$
$$6 \times 9 = \underline{54}$$
$$2214$$

Add together to give 2214 – which is similar to the estimate.

Here are some other written methods…

1. Grid Method

314 x 25 is roughly **300 x 25 = 7500**

x	300	10	4	
20	6000	200	80	6280
5	1500	50	20	+1570
				7850

This is close enough to the estimate **7850**

2. Short Multiplication

473 x 8 is roughly **450 x 10 = 4500**

$$473$$
$$\times \quad 8$$

400 x 8	3200
70 x 8	560
3 x 8	24
	3784

or better still…

Start with the units, 8 x 3 = 24. Put 4 down and carry over the 2 into the tens column.

8 x 7 = 56, plus the 2 carried over gives 58. Put 8 down and carry over the 5.

8 x 4 = 32 plus the 5 carried is 37, so put the 7 in the hundreds and 3 in the thousands column.

th	h	t	u
	4	7	3
X		5 2	8
3	7	8	4

3. Long Multiplication

Once the number you multiply gets bigger than 10 we need to use **long multiplication**.

564 x 23 is roughly **600 x 20 = 12000**

$$564$$
$$\times \quad 2\,3$$

(564 x 20)	11280
(564 x 3)	1692
	12972

Add the two multiplications together.

---

33 Try these using the short multiplication method:

a) 65 x 4   **b)** 73 x 6   **c)** 124 x 3
d) 563 x 6   **e)** 794 x 7   **f)** 438 x 9

34 Use any method you choose to work these out:

a) 63 x 24   **b)** 135 x 32   **c)** 273 x 45
d) 381 x 53   **e)** 624 x 76   **f)** 339 x 68

Numbers

Dividing – Written Methods

Always start by getting a rough estimate of the answer e.g. **184 ÷ 8** is between 160 ÷ 8 = 20 and 200 ÷ 8 = 25

1. Grouping

This is a method where you keep taking away multiples of the number you are dividing by. A good way to start is to take away multiples of 8. If we wanted to do the division above:

$$
\begin{array}{r}
184 \\
-\ 80 \quad \text{10 x 8} \\
\hline
104 \\
-\ 80 \quad \text{10 x 8} \\
\hline
24 \\
-\ 24 \quad \text{3 x 8} \\
\hline
0 \quad 23
\end{array}
$$

And so...
184 ÷ 8 = 23, which fits in with the rough estimate.

2. Short Division

352 ÷ 8 (or 8 into 352) is between 320 ÷ 8 = 40 and 400 ÷ 8 = 50

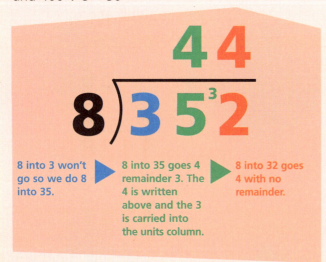

8 into 3 won't go so we do 8 into 35. ▶ 8 into 35 goes 4 remainder 3. The 4 is written above and the 3 is carried into the units column. ▶ 8 into 32 goes 4 with no remainder.

3. Long Division

736 ÷ 23 is roughly 720 ÷ 20 = 36

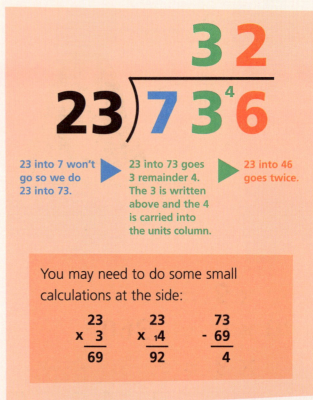

23 into 7 won't go so we do 23 into 73. ▶ 23 into 73 goes 3 remainder 4. The 3 is written above and the 4 is carried into the units column. ▶ 23 into 46 goes twice.

You may need to do some small calculations at the side:

$$
\begin{array}{r}
23 \\
\times\ 3 \\
\hline
69
\end{array}
\qquad
\begin{array}{r}
23 \\
\times\ {}_1 4 \\
\hline
92
\end{array}
\qquad
\begin{array}{r}
73 \\
-\ 69 \\
\hline
4
\end{array}
$$

OR

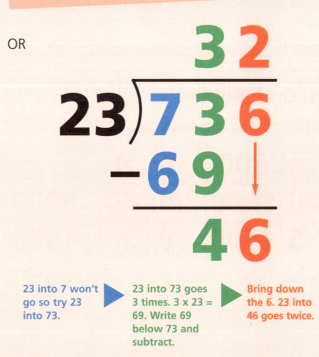

23 into 7 won't go so try 23 into 73. ▶ 23 into 73 goes 3 times. 3 x 23 = 69. Write 69 below 73 and subtract. ▶ Bring down the 6. 23 into 46 goes twice.

35 Try these using short division:
a) 423 ÷ 3   b) 365 ÷ 5   c) 513 ÷ 9
d) 636 ÷ 4   e) 732 ÷ 6   f) 812 ÷ 4

36 Try these using long division:
a) 350 ÷ 14   b) 648 ÷ 27   c) 756 ÷ 42
d) 728 ÷ 28   e) 527 ÷ 31   f) 968 ÷ 22

Multiplying and Dividing Decimals

You should be able to multiply and divide decimals by whole numbers. It is even more important when you do these to have a rough idea of the answer.

3.14×9 is roughly $3 \times 9 = 27$

$$
\begin{array}{l}
3.14 \times 9 \\
\hline
3.00 \times 9 = 27.00 \\
0.10 \times 9 = 0.90 \\
0.04 \times 9 = \underline{0.36} \\
28.26
\end{array}
$$

Keep the decimal points on top of each other

3.25×17 is roughly $3 \times 20 = 60$
This can be set out like a long multiplication.

Keep the digits in nice neat columns

$$
\begin{array}{r}
3.25 \\
\times 17_1 _3 \\
\hline
(3.25 \times 10) \quad 32.50 \\
(3.25 \times 7) \quad 22.75 \\
\hline
55.25
\end{array}
$$

The decimal point in the answer goes directly below the decimal point in the question.

$60.9 \div 7$ is between $56 \div 7 = 8$ and $63 \div 7 = 9$ and can be set out as a short division.

$$
\begin{array}{r}
8.7 \\
7\overline{)60.9}
\end{array}
$$

$86.4 \div 24$ is roughly $80 \div 20 = 4$
This can be set out as a long division.

$$
\begin{array}{r}
3.6 \\
24\overline{)86.4} \\
-72 \\
\hline
144
\end{array}
$$

$$
\begin{array}{cc}
24 & 24 \\
\times_1 3 & \times_2 6 \\
\hline
72 & 144
\end{array}
$$

---

37 Have a go at these:
a) 26.3×5 b) 1.54×8 c) 43.8×22
d) 3.63×41 e) 0.65×27 f) 88.2×39

38 Get a rough idea of the answer before starting on these…
a) $18.3 \div 3$ b) $3.68 \div 4$ c) $37.8 \div 14$
d) £945 $\div$ 35 e) $8.06 \div 26$ f) $94.5 \div 35$

Checking Your Answer

Since multiplying and dividing are **opposites**, you can use this to **check your answers**.

e.g. $28 \times 15 = 420$ and so…

If you have done a **multiplication**, check it with **division**.

$420 \div 15 = 28$
or
$420 \div 28 = 15$

39 Use an opposite to check these answers
a) $18 \times 7 = 136$ b) $135 \div 9 = 15$
c) $12 \times 11 = 132$ d) $9 \times 14 = 126$

40 Use opposites to help you find the missing numbers.
a) $8 \times \square = 192$ b) $\square \times 12 = 408$
c) $\square \div 11 = 198$ d) $364 \div \square = 26$

e.g. $46.8 \div 13 = 3.6$ and so…

If you have done a **division**, check it with **multiplication**.

$3.6 \times 13 = 46.8$

Numbers

Dividing – Remainders

The number we are dividing by doesn't always go exactly into the number we are dividing. We are left with a **remainder**. The remainder can be written down at the end, or better still, given as a **fraction**.

357 ÷ 8 is between
320 ÷ 8 = 40 and 400 ÷ 8 = 50

$$8\overline{)357}$$ = 44 remainder 5

8 goes into 37 4 times with 5 left over.

95 ÷ 7 is between
70 ÷ 7 = 10 and 140 ÷ 7 = 20

$$7\overline{)95}$$ = 13 r 4 = $13\frac{4}{7}$

We could even go into decimal fractions.
276 ÷ 8 is between
240 ÷ 8 = 30 and 320 ÷ 8 = 40

$$8\overline{)276.0}$$ = 34.5

Put an extra zero here. 8 goes into 40 5 times.

The decimal points go on top of each other.

365 ÷ 7 is between
350 ÷ 7 = 50 and 420 ÷ 7 = 60

$$7\overline{)365.0}$$ = 52.1

10 ÷ 7 is 1 remainder 3. We could put another zero and do 30 ÷ 7, but there would be another remainder. So it is sensible to stop here.

How we write the remainder depends on what we are being asked to do. We need to be clear about what the remainder means. Sometimes we need to round up or down.

Eggs are packed in boxes of six. A farmer collects 217 eggs in a week. How many boxes can he fill?

217 ÷ 6 is between
180 ÷ 6 = 30 and
240 ÷ 6 = 40

$$6\overline{)217}$$ = 36 r 1

So 36 boxes can be filled (with 1 egg left over). If the question had asked 'How many boxes are needed to put all the eggs into' the answer would be 37, because 36 would not be enough.

41 Find the remainder and give the answer with a fraction.
a) 254 ÷ 7   b) 463 ÷ 4
c) 312 ÷ 5   d) 269 ÷ 14
e) 365 ÷ 18   f) 584 ÷ 21

42 Write the answers to these with a decimal.
a) 130 ÷ 4   b) 147 ÷ 6
c) 250 ÷ 8   d) 177 ÷ 5
e) 183 ÷ 7   f) 256 ÷ 9

43 a) A taxi can hold 5 passengers. How many taxis will be needed for 73 passengers?
b) A ribbon is 160cm long. How many pieces 12cm long can be cut from it and how much will be left over?

Calculations – Negative Numbers

On a cold morning, the temperature at 8 o'clock was -2°C. But as the Sun came up, the temperature rose by 6°C. Counting up on the thermometer, the temperature went up to 4°C. This can be written as -2 + 6 = 4°C.

As the Sun went down in the evening, the temperature went down by 9°C. Counting down on the thermometer, the temperature went down to -5°C. This can be written as 4 – 9 = -5°C.

Make a copy of one of the thermometers opposite and use it to help you answer these questions:

Morning **Midday** **Evening**

 44 What is the new temperature if:
  a) It starts at -3°C and goes up by 5°C
  b) It starts at -4°C and goes up by 7°C
  c) It starts at -5°C and goes up by 3°C
  d) It starts at 1°C and goes down by 2°C
  e) It starts at 5°C and goes down by 10°C

 45 **a)** The temperature rises from -2°C to 5°C. By how much has it gone up?
  b) The temperature falls from 4°C to -1°C. By how much has it gone down?
  c) The temperature falls from -1°C to -4°C. By how much has it gone down?

Negative numbers can be used for things other than temperature. If you have -£5, you owe £5. If a height of 20m above sea level is written 20m, then -15m means 15m below sea level.

Whatever the meaning of the negative numbers, we need to be able to add or subtract with them.

It is helpful to think about moving along the number line. When **adding**, count to the **right**, when **subtracting** count to the **left**.

20 m

-15 m

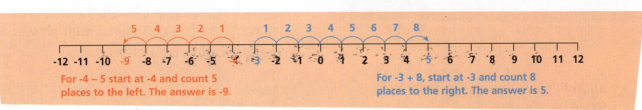

For -4 – 5 start at -4 and count 5 places to the left. The answer is -9.

For -3 + 8, start at -3 and count 8 places to the right. The answer is 5.

If you try calculating 3 – 8 on your calculator, it should give the answer as -5. Sometimes the '-' sign appears after the 5 as 5-, and sometimes it appears at the beginning of the display. Try this on your calculator and make sure you know where the '-' sign appears.

 46 Use a number line to help you work out:
  a) 10 – 12   **b)** -5 + 11   **c)** 2 – 8
  d) -7 + 4   **e)** -3 – 7   **f)** 1 – 4

Numbers

Multiples

The multiples of **3** are **3**, **6**, **9**, **12**, **15**… and so on. They are the numbers in the **3** times table. The first five multiples of **7** are the first five numbers in the **7** times table. They are **7**, **14**, **21**, **28** and **35**.

The multiples of 2 are **even numbers** 2, 4, 6, 8, 10… All the others are **odd numbers** 1, 3, 5, 7, 9…

Some Useful Tips

1 Many multiples have patterns which makes finding them easier.
Multiples of 2 always end in 2, 4, 6, 8 or 0.
Multiples of 5 always end in 5 or 0.
Multiples of 10 always end in 0.

> 420 is a multiple of 2, 5 and 10

2 If the digits in a number add up to a multiple of 3, then the number is a multiple of 3.
The digits of **261** add up to give
2 + **6** + **1** = **9** which is a multiple of 3, so 261 is a multiple of 3.
If an even number is a multiple of 3, it is also a multiple of 6.

> 114 is a multiple of 3 and 6

47
a) Write down the first five multiples of 8.
b) Which of these numbers are multiples of 5?
    i) 35 **ii)** 157 **iii)** 240 **iv)** 475 **v)** 554
c) Which of these numbers are multiples of 3 and 6?
    i) 34 **ii)** 96 **iii)** 252 **iv)** 610 **v)** 1026

Lowest Common Multiple

The multiples of **4** are: **4, 8, 12, 16, 20, 24**…
The multiples of **6** are: **6, 12, 18, 24, 30**…

12 and **24** are **common multiples** of **4** and **6**.

Since, **12** is the smallest it is called the **lowest common multiple** of **4** and **6**.

48
a) Find the lowest common multiple of 5 and 7.
b) Find the lowest common multiple of 6 and 15.

Factors

The **factors** of a number are all the numbers that go into it **exactly**.

The factors of 8 are 1, 2, 4 and 8. The factors of 30 are 1, 2, 3, 5, 6, 10, 15 and 30.

When we are finding all the **factors** of a number it is useful to pair them up. 3 is a factor of 42, 42 ÷ 3 = 14, so 14 is also a factor of 42. The factors of 42 are…

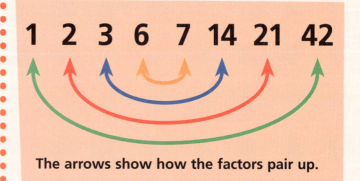

1 2 3 6 7 14 21 42

The arrows show how the factors pair up.

It is quite common to get **multiple** and **factor** mixed up. So be careful. Think of **multiples** as the **multiplication** table of the number.

49 Find all the factors of:
a) 12 b) 20 c) 32 d) 25 e) 17

50 25 has an odd number of factors. Which other numbers between 1 and 40 have an odd number of factors?

Square Numbers

The numbers **1**, **4**, **9**, **16**, **25** and **36** are the first six **square numbers**.

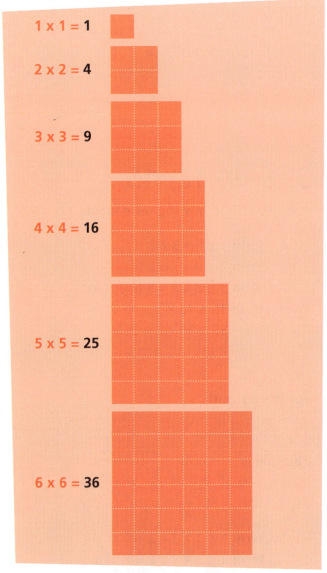

1 x 1 = 1

2 x 2 = 4

3 x 3 = 9

4 x 4 = 16

5 x 5 = 25

6 x 6 = 36

If we **multiply** a **whole number** by itself we get a **square number**.

7 x 7 = 49, so 49 is a **square number**.
18 x 18 = 324, so 324 is a **square number**.

We can write 18 x 18 as 18^2. This is pronounced '18 squared'.

51 Calculate the first 12 square numbers. You need to learn these.

52 What is...
a) 8^2 b) 12^2 c) 15^2 d) 20^2

53 Which number, when multiplied by itself, gives a) 169 b) 289

Prime Numbers

Numbers that only have **two factors** are called **prime numbers**. The factors of a prime number are **itself** and **one**. 31 is a prime number as it can only be divided by 31 and 1.

It is worth trying to memorise the prime numbers that are less than 20. They are **2**, **3**, **5**, **7**, **11**, **13**, **17** and **19**.

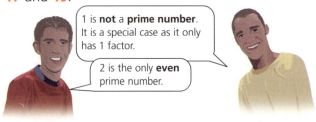

1 is **not** a **prime number**. It is a special case as it only has 1 factor.

2 is the only **even** prime number.

54 Write down all the numbers from 21 to 100. Cross out all the multiples of 2 (the even numbers), then 3, then 5 and finally 7. Put a circle around the numbers that are not crossed out – these are all **prime**.

Prime Factors

Factors of a number that are prime numbers are called **prime factors**. These can easily be found using a **factor tree**.

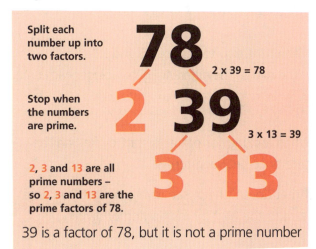

Split each number up into two factors.

78

2 x 39 = 78

Stop when the numbers are prime.

2 39

3 x 13 = 39

2, 3 and 13 are all prime numbers – so 2, 3 and 13 are the prime factors of 78.

3 13

39 is a factor of 78, but it is not a prime number

Writing down all the prime numbers as a multiplication gives: **2 x 3 x 13 = 78**

55 Find the prime factors of a) 30 b) 70 c) 84 d) 36. Write them out as a multiplication to check.

Numbers

Number Patterns

In the number pattern **2**, **5**, **8**, **11**, **14**…

2 is called the **first term**

5 is called the **second term**

8 is called the **third term**

… and so on.

Spotting patterns is very important. We need to be able to continue the pattern, writing down the **next** two or three **terms**. We also need to be able to **describe** to someone what the pattern is. Usually it is easier to give the **rule** for how to get from one term to the next.

2, 6, 10, 14, 18…
+4 +4 +4 +4

The next three terms are 22, 26 and 30.
The rule is 'Add 4 each time.'

1, 3, 9, 27…
x3 x3 x3

The next two terms are 81 and 243.
The rule is 'Multiply by 3 each time.'

1, 3, 6, 10…
+2 +3 +4

The next two terms are 15 and 21.
The rule is 'The difference gets 1 bigger each time.'

When looking for patterns start by finding the difference between terms.

If that doesn't help, see if you can get from one term to the next by multiplying or dividing.

Sometimes we may have to find the rule for getting from one term to the next. At other times we may need to know the 15th term or even the 85th term! It is quicker to use a rule that links the number to its **term number**.

For the pattern:

3, 6, 9, 12, 15…

The rule is 'Multiply the term number by 3'

term 1 is 1 x 3 = **3**
term 2 is 2 x 3 = **6**
term 3 is 3 x 3 = **9** and so on…
so term 15 is 15 x 3 = **45**
and term 85 is 85 x 3 = **255**

For the pattern:

5, 8, 11, 14, 17…

The rule is 'Multiply the term number by 3 then add 2' (It is the same as the pattern above, but each term is 2 bigger)

term 1 is 1 x 3 + 2 = **5**
term 2 is 2 x 3 + 2 = **8**
term 3 is 3 x 3 + 2 = **11** and so on…
so term 15 is 15 x 3 + 2 = **47**
and term 85 is 85 x 3 + 2 = **257**

56 For each pattern find the next 2 terms and give the rule.

a) 1, 4, 7, 10… **e)** 1, 2, 4, 7, 11…
b) 15, 13, 11, 9… **f)** 1, 4, 9, 16…
c) 2, 6, 18, 54… **g)** 8, 15, 22, 29…
d) 256, 64, 16… **h)** 1, 2, 5, 10, 17…

57 For each pattern find the 15th term, the 85th term and give the rule.

a) 4, 8, 12, 16, 20…
b) 7, 14, 21, 28, 35…
c) 5, 9, 13, 17, 21…
d) 6, 13, 20, 27, 34…

Formulas

Formulas are a useful way of giving the **rule** that connects two numbers. Here is a pattern made from **red** and **blue** tiles.

For each pattern:
Number of blue tiles = Diagram number + 1
Number of red tiles = (2 x Diagram number) + 8

So in diagram number 4:
Number of **blue** tiles = 4 + 1 = 5
Number of **red** tiles = (2 x 4) + 8 = 16

And in diagram number 17:
Number of **blue** tiles = 17 + 1 = 18
Number of **red** tiles = (2 x 17) + 8 = 42

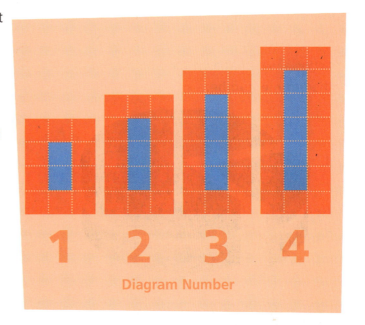

Diagram Number

---

58 In diagram number 20:
a) How many blue tiles will there be?
b) How many red tiles will there be?
c) How many tiles will there be altogether?

d) Copy and complete this formula:
Number of tiles altogether =
.... **x Diagram number +** ....

Here is a pattern made from matchsticks:

The rule is:
number of matchsticks = (2 x diagram number) + 1
It is quicker to just write **m = (2 x n) + 1**

So in pattern number 4,
n = 4 so, m = (2 x 4) + 1 = 9

And in pattern number 17,
n = 17 so, m = (2 x 17) + 1 = 35

Using letters instead of numbers is **algebra**.
In **algebra** we avoid using '**x**' signs.
Instead of **2 x n**, it is better to write **2n**.
The rule is now **m = 2n + 1**

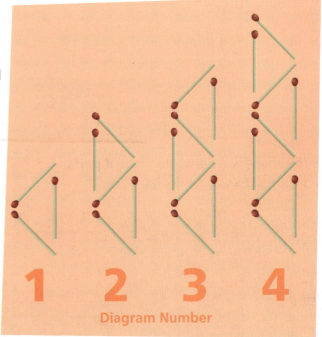

Diagram Number

---

59 For the rule m = 2n + 1. Find m when:
a) n = 5   b) n = 15   c) n = 75

60 In a different pattern, the rule is m = 4n – 2.
Find m when: a) n = 1   b) n = 7   c) n = 15

Numbers

Fractions

If we cut a cake into 5 equal slices, each slice is $\frac{1}{5}$ **(one fifth)** of the cake. Two slices will be $\frac{2}{5}$.

A fraction always has a **whole number** on top of another **whole number**.

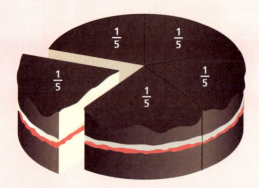

Any fraction can be shown in a diagram by dividing a shape up into the number of equal pieces given by the bottom number (**denominator**) and shading in the number of parts given by the top number (**numerator**).

This shape is divided into **8 equal parts**, 2 parts are shaded. So the fraction is $\frac{2}{8}$

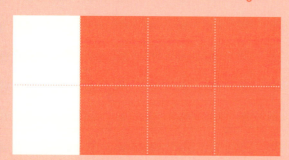

This shape is divided into **4 equal parts**, 1 part is shaded. So the fraction is $\frac{1}{4}$

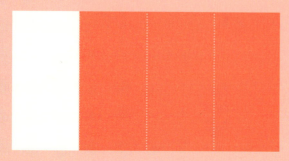

These two fractions are the **same amount**. They are **equivalent**. $\frac{2}{8}$ is **equivalent** to $\frac{1}{4}$. We can write $\frac{2}{8} = \frac{1}{4}$

If you multiply (or divide) the top and bottom numbers of any fraction by the **same amount**, you create a new fraction that is **equivalent** to the fraction that you started with.

$$\frac{2}{5} = \frac{6}{15} \qquad \frac{18}{24} = \frac{3}{4}$$

To find how many eighths is the same as $\frac{3}{4}$, we need to work out what we multiply 4 by to get 8, and then multiply the 3 by the same amount.

$$\frac{3}{4} = \frac{6}{8}$$

x2 here...

... because you need to x2 here

To find how many twelfths is the same as $\frac{3}{4}$, we would need to work out what we multiply 4 by to get 12 and then do the same to the 3.

$$\frac{3}{4} = \frac{9}{12}$$

x3 here...

... because you need to x3 here

61 What fraction of each shape is shaded blue?

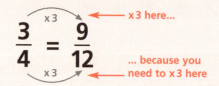

a)

b)

c)

d)

62 Find the missing numbers:

a) $\frac{1}{2} = \frac{}{8}$ b) $\frac{4}{5} = \frac{}{30}$

c) $\frac{3}{2} = \frac{}{20}$ d) $\frac{}{9} = \frac{2}{3}$

e) $\frac{}{20} = \frac{3}{2}$ f) $\frac{4}{7} = \frac{}{35}$

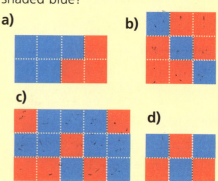

Simplifying Fractions

When you divide the **numerator** (top number) and **denominator** (bottom number) by the same amount, they get smaller – this is called simplifying the fraction, or cancelling down.

$$\frac{45}{60} \overset{\div 5}{\underset{\div 5}{=}} \frac{9}{12} \overset{\div 3}{\underset{\div 3}{=}} \frac{3}{4}$$

All of these fractions are equivalent. 3 and 4 cannot be divided any further by the same amount. $\frac{3}{4}$ is the simplest form of these fractions.

Mixed Numbers

Mixed numbers have a whole part and a fraction part. Such as:

Whole part → $4\frac{3}{8}$ ← Fraction part

It is useful sometimes to be able to write a mixed number as a top heavy, or improper fraction. Since there are 8 eighths in a whole one, there are 32 eighths in four whole ones, and so...

Mixed number $4\frac{3}{8} = \frac{32}{8} + \frac{3}{8} = \frac{35}{8}$ Improper fraction

Sometimes it is useful to do this the other way, to write an improper fraction as a mixed number.

$$\frac{23}{8} = 2\frac{7}{8}$$

8 goes into **23**, **2** times with **7** left over.

Comparing Fractions

Which is the biggest, $\frac{3}{4}$ or $\frac{2}{3}$? We can answer this by using:

1 **A number line**

Find $\frac{1}{4}$s by dividing from **0** to **1** into **4** equal parts.

Find $\frac{1}{3}$s by dividing from **0** to **1** into **3** equal parts.

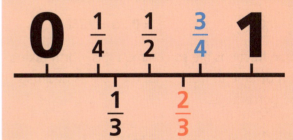

$\frac{3}{4}$ is bigger than $\frac{2}{3}$ as it is further to the right on the number line.

2 **Common denominators**

$$\frac{3}{4} \overset{\times 3}{\underset{\times 3}{=}} \frac{9}{12} \qquad \frac{2}{3} \overset{\times 4}{\underset{\times 4}{=}} \frac{8}{12}$$

$\frac{9}{12}$ is bigger than $\frac{8}{12}$

so, $\frac{3}{4}$ is bigger than $\frac{2}{3}$

---

63 Write these fractions in their simplest form.
a) $\frac{8}{12}$ b) $\frac{10}{16}$ c) $\frac{5}{15}$ d) $\frac{21}{28}$

64 Write these fractions as mixed numbers.
a) $\frac{11}{8}$ b) $\frac{23}{10}$ c) $\frac{24}{5}$ d) $\frac{12}{8}$

65 Which of these fractions is the largest?
a) $\frac{1}{3}$ or $\frac{2}{5}$ b) $\frac{5}{6}$ or $\frac{3}{4}$ c) $\frac{13}{8}$ or $\frac{5}{3}$

Numbers

Percentages

A **percentage** is just a particular type of fraction. A percentage is a fraction where the denominator (bottom number) is 100. The symbol for percent is **%**.

$$\frac{36}{100} \text{ is written as } 36\%$$

So if a fraction is written with a denominator of 100, the numerator (top number) is the percentage.

$$\frac{3}{4} \overset{\times 25}{\underset{\times 25}{=}} \frac{75}{100} \quad \text{so} \quad \frac{3}{4} = 75\%$$

$\frac{75}{100}$ can also be easily written as a decimal.

$$\frac{75}{100} = 0.75 \quad \text{so} \quad \frac{3}{4} = 0.75 = 75\%$$

Some fractions are so common it is worth taking a bit of time to learn what they are as decimals and percentages.

$$\frac{1}{4} = 0.25 = 25\%$$
$$\frac{1}{2} = 0.5 = 50\%$$
$$\frac{3}{4} = 0.75 = 75\% \text{ ... and so on}$$

$$\frac{1}{10} = 0.1 = 10\%$$
$$\frac{2}{10} = 0.2 = 20\%$$
$$\frac{3}{10} = 0.3 = 30\% \text{ ... and so on}$$

$$\frac{1}{100} = 0.01 = 1\%$$
$$\frac{2}{100} = 0.02 = 2\%$$
$$\frac{35}{100} = 0.35 = 35\% \text{ ... and so on}$$

Number Lines

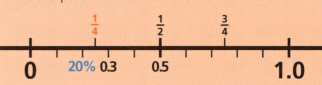

Here is part of a number line

Zero to one is divided into ten equal parts, so each part is $\frac{1}{10}$ or 0.1 or 10%.

Thinking about where you would place a fraction, decimal or percentage on the number line will help you to place them in order

$\frac{1}{4}$ is to the right of **20%**, so $\frac{1}{4}$ is bigger than **20%**.

$\frac{1}{4}$ is to the left of **0.3**, so $\frac{1}{4}$ is smaller than **0.3**.

Comparing the size of a mixture of fractions, decimals and percentages is usually done most easily by changing them all into percentages – which is why teachers like to give exam marks as percentages.

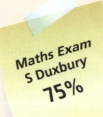

Maths Exam
S Duxbury
75%

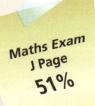

Maths Exam
J Page
51%

Maths Exam
R Plant
47%

Maths Exam
J P Jones
38%

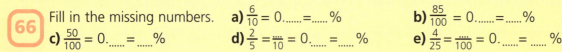

66 Fill in the missing numbers.   **a)** $\frac{6}{10} = 0.\text{......} = \text{......}\%$ **b)** $\frac{85}{100} = 0.\text{......} = \text{......}\%$ **c)** $\frac{50}{100} = 0.\text{......} = \text{......}\%$ **d)** $\frac{2}{5} = \frac{\text{....}}{10} = 0.\text{......} = \text{......}\%$ **e)** $\frac{4}{25} = \frac{\text{....}}{100} = 0.\text{......} = \text{......}\%$

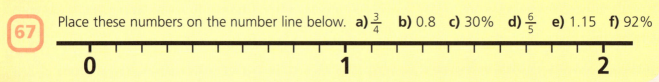

67 Place these numbers on the number line below.   **a)** $\frac{3}{4}$ **b)** 0.8   **c)** 30%   **d)** $\frac{6}{5}$ **e)** 1.15   **f)** 92%

0   1   2

Finding a Fraction of an Amount

To find $\frac{1}{4}$ of £60, divide it into 4 equal amounts:

$$60 \div 4 = 15$$

£60 =

$$\frac{1}{4} \text{ of } £60 = £15$$

$\frac{3}{4}$ of £60, will be 3 of these amounts:

$$3 \times 15 = 45$$

£60 =

$$\frac{3}{4} \text{ of } £60 = £45$$

To find a fraction of an amount:
Divide the amount by the **bottom** number and then **multiply** by the **top** number.

$\frac{7}{8}$ of 40 = 40 ÷ 8 × 7 = 5 × 7 = 35

SALE $\frac{1}{3}$ **OFF**

$\frac{1}{3}$ of £60 is £20, so that's £20 off!

Finding a Percentage of an Amount

There are a few different methods you could use here. You need to remember that
10% $= \frac{1}{10}$ which is found by **dividing by 10**, and **1%** $= \frac{1}{100}$ which is found by **dividing by 100**.

Example 1: To find 15% of 80,

work out 10% of 80 = **8**
and then 5% of 80 = $\frac{1}{2}$ of 8 = **4**
(Because 5% is half of 10%)
15% of 80 = **8** + **4**
= **12**

Example 2: To find 23% of £80,

work out 10% of £80 = **£8**
and 1% of £80 = **£0.80**

and then 20% of £80 = **£16**
and 3% of £80 = **£2.40**
23% of £80 = **£16** + **£2.40**
= **£18.40**

You can also use the percentage key on a calculator. To do this...

... press **80** 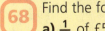 **23** to give you the answer.

Whenever you use a calculator to work out an answer that has units you should always think about the meaning of the digits given on the calculator display. In this example, the answer is an amount of money, so **18.4** on the calculator means **£18.40**.

---

68 Find the following amounts:
a) $\frac{1}{10}$ of £50   b) $\frac{3}{10}$ of £50   c) $\frac{2}{7}$ of 35kg
d) $\frac{9}{20}$ of 60p   e) $\frac{8}{15}$ of 90m

69 Find the following amounts:
a) 20% of £30   b) 75% of 18kg
c) 15% of £34   d) 42% of 67m

Numbers

Proportions and Ratios

Richard has **10 counters**, **4** are red and **6** are blue.

The proportion of the counters that are red can be given:

1   **as a fraction:** $\frac{4}{10}$ or $\frac{2}{5}$ of the counters are red.

2   **as a decimal: 0.4** of the counters are red.

3   **as a percentage: 40%** of the counters are red.

4   **in words:** '**4** in **10**' or '**2** in every **5**' or '**4** out of **10**' counters are red.

5   **as a ratio:** the ratio of red counters to blue counters is **4** to **6**. This can also be written as '**2** to **3**', '**2** to every **3**' or **2:3**.

All of these ways of describing the proportion of red counters can be used. They are all connected, they are all equivalent. It is very important to be careful with the words used, because **4** to **6** means the same as **4** in **10**.

Equivalent ratios can be found in the same way as equivalent fractions, and ratios can be simplified in the same way that fractions can be simplified.

In a class of 30 children, there are 20 girls and 10 boys. This means that there are 2 girls to every 1 boy.

Percentage of the Rest

In question 70, you should have put that **75%** of the vehicles were cars.

All the vehicles in the survey correspond to **100%**, and because **75** + **25** = **100**, then **25%** of the vehicles are not cars.

If **42%** of a class are girls, then **58%** must be boys, because **42** + **58** = **100**, and all of the class must be girls or boys.

If **80%** of pupils walk to school, then **20%** do not walk, but without any more information, we cannot say what percentage came by bus or by car or by bike.

---

70   Laura did a survey of 100 vehicles going past her school. 75 of the vehicles were cars, the others were vans, lorries and buses.

    a) What is the ratio of cars to other vehicles?

    b) What percentage of the vehicles were cars?

71   **a)** If 65% of a class have done their homework, what percentage have not?

    b) If 15% of teachers have holes in their socks, what percentage do not have holes in their socks?

Solving Problems

When you want to solve a problem you should always read the question through **twice**. Think about what you know already and what else you may need to work out to calculate the answer to the problem.

A girl goes into a shop. She buys a comic that costs 45p, a bar of candy for 28p and a can of cola for 55p. She pays with a £5 note. How much does she pay altogether, and how much change should she get from a £5 note?

Add together the cost of the three articles:
    45 + 28 + 55 = 128p

Then **subtract** this amount from £5:
    500 − 128 = 372p = £3.72

Answer: She spends £1.28 and she should get £3.72 change.

Always make sure that the **units** are the **same**.

72 For each question, write down the calculations and make sure your answer is clear.

   a) Four friends share £3.36 between them. How much do they each get?

   b) Six boxes weigh 13kg each. How much less than 80kg is the total weight?

   c) Two bags of raisins and an apple cost 75p. One bag of raisins and an apple cost 45p. How much does an apple cost?

Sometimes, you may be given a question where you need to use some of the information from the first part of the question to answer the second part. For example, Mrs Clarke buys some tennis balls. What is the cost of 1 box containing 6 tennis balls?

TENNIS BALLS

40p EACH

The calculation needed is **40 x 6 = 240p**.

Always write down the **calculation** you do.

We also need to make sure that the answer is sensible and helpful. Rather than giving the answer as **240p**, it is better to change it into pounds. 1 box of tennis balls will cost **£2.40**.

£7.00

Mrs Clarke buys boxes of tennis balls and shuttlecocks for the P.E. cupboard. She spends exactly £26.00. If she buys 5 boxes of tennis balls, how many boxes of shuttlecocks does she buy?

Cost of tennis balls is **£2.40 x 5 = £12**.

She spends **£26 − £12 = £14** on shuttlecocks. Each box of shuttlecocks cost **£7**.

Number of boxes bought = $\frac{£14}{£7}$ = 2

73 How many boxes of tennis balls does Mrs Clarke buy if she buys 3 boxes of shuttlecocks and spends £30.60 in total.

Numbers

Estimating

Some numbers cannot be given exactly. The number of hairs on your head for example.

1037
1038...

If you can't find, or don't need an exact number, you **estimate** it. Estimating is clever guessing, and the cleverer the guess, the better the estimate. Below are three methods you could use.

1 **Comparing To Known Amounts**
The label tells us that the jar holds **360** wine gums when it is full. We can estimate that the jar is a bit more than half full. $\frac{1}{2}$ **of 360 = 180**, so we can estimate that there are **200** wine gums in the jar.

2 **Having A System**
To estimate the number of 10p coins in a stack 1 metre high, we need a system. If there are **six** **10p** coins in a stack **1cm** high (and **100**cm = 1m) we can estimate that there will be **6 x 100 = 600 coins**

3 **Dividing Up**
Although the number line has not been divided up for you, there is no reason why you can't do it yourself. The arrow is about $\frac{1}{3}$ of the way between **0** and **-100** so we can estimate that the line is at **-35**.

-100   **0**

Rounding

Some numbers are given too accurately. It is often more sensible to **round** the number off to the nearest 10, 100 or 1000.

The number of people in my village is **3476**

3400 3410 3420 3430 3440 3450 3460 3470 3480 3490 3500
3476
3476 is closer to 3480 than 3470

To the nearest **10**   : 3476 rounds to **3480**
100 : 3476 rounds to **3500**
1000 : 3476 rounds to **3000**

3497 is 3500 to the nearest 10 and to the nearest 100.

Dividing with a calculator often gives answers with lots of digits after the decimal point. If we divide 47 by the 11 the answer is 4.2727272.

4   4.1   4.2   4.3
4.2727272 is between 4.2 and 4.3 It is closer to 4.3

To the nearest whole number:
4.2727272 rounds to 4
To the nearest tenth:
4.2727272 rounds to 4.3
To **one decimal place**.
4.2727272 rounds to 4.3

74
a) Estimate the length of a line of 500 1p coins.
b) Estimate the number of words in this book.
c) If the jar of wine gums above held 500 sweets when full, estimate the number of sweets that have been taken out.

75 Round:
a) 13372 to the nearest 100
b) 10433 to the nearest 1000
c) 17.3131 to the nearest whole number
d) 8.181818 to the nearest tenth

Co-ordinates

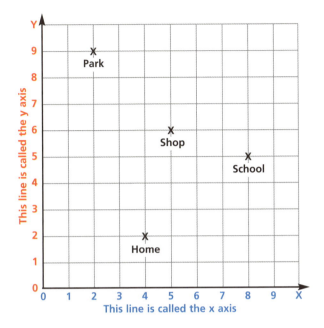

Co-ordinates are used to give the position of something on a grid.

The position of Home is **4** on the **x axis** and **2** on the **y axis**. This is written (**4**,**2**)

Called the x co-ordinate   Called the y co-ordinate

The School is at (**8**,**5**), the Shop is at (**5**,**6**), the Park is at (**2**,**9**)

Remember: The x axis always goes across the page, because x is a cross!

And always:

- Write the x co-ordinate first and then the y co-ordinate (it's in alphabetical order).
- Put the numbers in a bracket.
- Put a comma in between them.

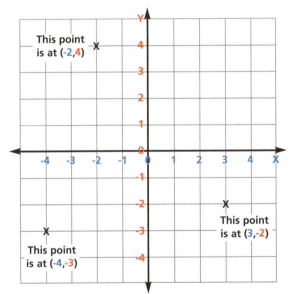

The points can also be on the other side of the axes. Negative numbers are used to tell on which side of the axes the points lie.

76 Make a copy of the grid at the top of the page, then plot the following points joining them up as you go along.
(**2**,**1**) (**8**,**1**) (**8**,**7**) (**5**,**9**) (**2**,**7**) (**2**,**1**)

77 Make a copy of the grid in the middle of the page, then plot these points:
(**-3**,**4**) (**4**,**-3**) (**-2**,**-2**) (**-1**,**3**) (**3**,**-1**) (**-3**,**-1**)

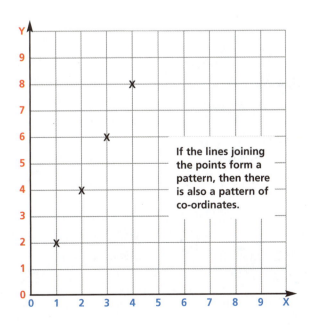

If the lines joining the points form a pattern, then there is also a pattern of co-ordinates.

- These points are in a straight line.
- They have co-ordinates (**1**,**2**) (**2**,**4**) (**3**,**6**) (**4**,**8**).
- The y co-ordinate is always 2 times the x co-ordinate.
- The point at (**6**,**12**) would also be on this line because it fits the pattern.
- The point at (**8**,**4**) would not be on the line because it does not fit the pattern.

78 Which of these points fit the pattern of the grid at the bottom of the page?
(**9**,**15**) (**7**,**14**) (**14**,**7**) (**2.5**,**5**)

Shape, Space and Measures

Describing Shapes

Imagine trying to describe a shape to a friend over the phone.

It's got 4 sides

The **number** of **sides** is important.

All the sides are **straight**

Sides can be **curved** or **straight**. **Curved sides** can be **concave** (go in like a cave) or **convex**

The sides opposite each other are **parallel**

Parallel lines are always the same distance apart, they never meet.

Two of the sides are much **longer** than the other two

This shape is a **Parallelogram**

Polygons

Shapes whose **sides** are **all straight** are **polygons** ('Poly' means many). Some important **polygons** have their own names:

A polygon with: **3** sides is a **triangle**.
　　　　　　　　4 sides is a **quadrilateral**.
　　　　　　　　5 sides is a **pentagon**.
　　　　　　　　6 sides is a **hexagon**.
　　　　　　　　7 sides is a **heptagon**.
　　　　　　　　8 sides is an **octagon**.
　　　　　　　　(You should learn these names)

If all the **sides** are the **same length** and all the **angles** the **same size**, then the polygon is a **regular polygon**.

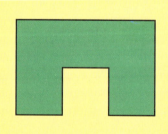

This shape has 8 sides so it is an **octagon**.

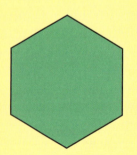

This shape has 6 equal sides. All the angles are the same, so it is a **regular hexagon**.

1 For each shape, either say what type of polygon it is or explain why it is not a polygon.

a)   b)   c)   d)

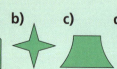

2 Which of the shapes opposite have a pair of parallel sides?

Shape, Space and Measures

Triangles

Triangles are either:

Equilateral
All 3 sides are the **same length**. All angles are the same size.

Isosceles
2 of the sides are the **same length**. 2 angles are the same.

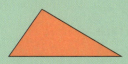

Scalene
All the sides have **different lengths**. All angles are different.

Right Angled
One angle is a **right angle**.

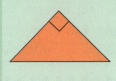

Isosceles triangles can be right angled.

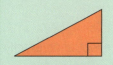

Scalene triangles can be right angled.

Isosceles is a Greek word meaning 'equal legs'.

Quadrilaterals

Some important **quadrilaterals** have their own names.

Square
All **sides** are the **same length**. All **angles** are **right angles**. A special rectangle.

Rectangle
All **angles** are **right angles**. Opposite sides are parallel and equal. A special parallelogram.

Parallelogram
Opposite sides are **parallel** and **equal**.

Rhombus
All **sides** are the **same length**. A special parallelogram.

Trapezium
One pair of **sides** is **parallel**.

Kite
Two **pairs** of **adjacent sides** are the **same length**.

Diagonals of a Quadrilateral

Lines that go from one corner of a quadrilateral to the opposite corner are called **diagonals**. All quadrilaterals have **two** diagonals. For a rhombus the diagonals cross or **intersect** at right angles. The intersection is in the middle of each diagonal. We can say the diagonals **bisect** each other – they cut each other in half.

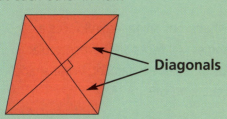

Diagonals

In different quadrilaterals, the diagonals do not always intersect at right angles, and the diagonals do not always bisect each other.

3 Draw a square, a rectangle, a parallelogram, a trapezium and kite. Draw the diagonals on each shape.
a) Which of these shapes have diagonals which meet at right angles?
b) Which of these shapes have diagonals which bisect each other?

Shape, Space and Measures

3-Dimensional Shapes

Solids are **3-dimensional** (3-D) shapes. A **solid** has thickness. It is not flat like a piece of paper. 3-D shapes can have **faces**, **edges** and **corners**.

A cube is a 3-D shape.

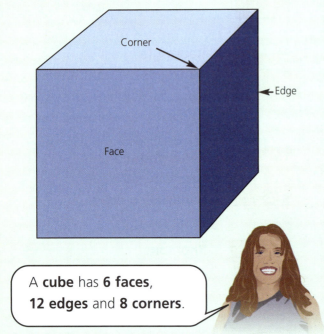

Corner

Edge

Face

A **cube** has **6 faces**, **12 edges** and **8 corners**.

These shapes are all types of **pyramid**. The first one is a **cone**.

Sphere

Hemisphere

This shape is called a **sphere** and half a sphere is called a **hemisphere**.

Faces can be **flat** or **curved**. Two **faces** meet along an **edge**. **Edges** can be **straight** or **curved**. **Edges** meet at a **corner** (or **vertex**).

A **cylinder** has **1 curved face** and **2 flat faces**.

This pyramid has **4 triangular faces** and **1 square face**.

It can be helpful to mention if a shape has **parallel faces**. Faces that meet at right angles can be described as **perpendicular faces**.

Polyhedrons

If all the faces of a 3-D shape are polygons, the shape is a **polyhedron**.

This shape has six rectangular faces, and two hexagonal faces. All the faces are polygons, so it is a polyhedron.

A polyhedron with **4 faces** is called a **tetrahedron**.

A polyhedron with **8 faces** is called an **octahedron**.

A polyhedron with **12 faces** is called a **dodecahedron**.

Prisms

If this shape was sliced up, each slice would be exactly the same shape and size – it has a '**constant cross section**.' Any shape that can be sliced up like this is called a **prism**. This shape is a **triangular prism**.

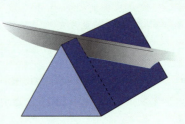

Cubes, cuboids and cylinders are all types of prism.

4

I am thinking of a shape...

a) This shape has five faces. One is a square and four are triangles. No faces are parallel. What shape am I thinking of?

b) This shape has six faces. All faces are rectangles. All faces are perpendicular. Opposite faces are parallel. What shape am I thinking of?

Angles

An **angle** is a measure of **rotation** or **turn**. It is the difference in **direction** between two straight lines. We can measure angles as a **fraction** of a **whole turn**.

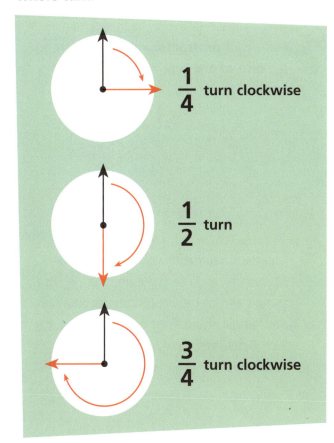

$\frac{1}{4}$ turn clockwise

$\frac{1}{2}$ turn

$\frac{3}{4}$ turn clockwise

A more **accurate** way of measuring an angle is to use **degrees**. There are **360 degrees** in a **full turn**. 360 degrees is written 360°.

People used to think the Earth took 360 days to go around the Sun.

Types of Angle

Acute
An angle that is **less than 90°** is called an **acute angle**.

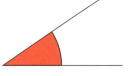

Right
A 90° angle is called a **right angle**. A little square is used to indicate a right angle.

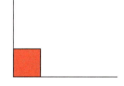

Obtuse
An angle that is **between 90° and 180°** is called an **obtuse angle**.

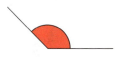

Reflex
An angle that is **between 180° and 360°** is called a **reflex angle**.

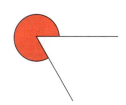

5 For each shape below, write down how many acute, right, obtuse and reflex angles it has inside it.

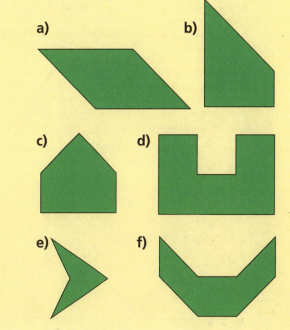

a)

b)

c)

d)

e)

f)

Shape, Space and Measures

Measuring Angles

Angles are measured using a **protractor** or **angle measurer**. A protractor has two zeros to measure from.

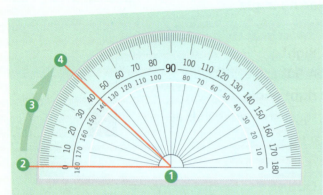

To measure an angle:

1 Place the centre of the protractor at the point where the two lines meet.

2 Put one of the **zeros** on the protractor on one of the lines of the angle.

3 Measure the angle using the scale with the **zero** on it that you have used.

4 The angle is 43°.

This angle is between 110° and 120°. It is 3° past 110 so the angle is 113°

Because we are using this zero, we use the inside scale

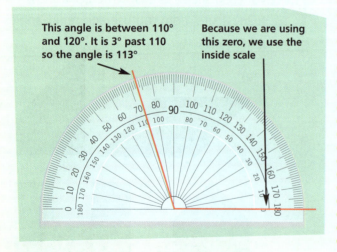

Drawing Angles

To draw an angle of 77°:

1 Start by drawing a straight line. Always use a **sharp** pencil.

_____

2 Place your **protractor** with the **centre** at the **end of the line** where you want to draw the angle.

3 Make a small mark with your pencil at 77°. Make sure you use the correct scale. You should aim to be as accurate as possible. Your angle should not be more than 1 or 2 degrees out.

4 Remove your protractor and draw a line between the end of the line and the mark you made.

6 Measure these angles:
a)   b)

7 Draw these angles accurately.
a)   b)
40°   156°

Calculating Angles

It is difficult to measure the size of an angle exactly. Sometimes we can calculate the size of an angle instead, this is usually quicker and more accurate.

Look out for questions that ask you to 'calculate the angle' – you must not try to find the answer by measuring the angle.

Angles At a Point

The angles at a point add up to 360°, because they make up a full turn and there are 360° in a full turn.

120° 150° a

a + 120° + 150° = 360°, so...
a = 360° − 270° (120° + 150° = 270°)
a = 90°

Angles On a Straight Line

Angles on a straight line add up to 180°.

20° b 30°

b + 20° + 30° = 180°, so...
b = 180° − 50° (20° + 30° = 50°)
b = 130°

Angles In a Triangle

Cut out any triangle. Tear it into 3 pieces with a corner in each. You should be able to put the corners together to make a straight line.
So, the angles in a triangle add up to 180°

c 50° 80°

c + 50° + 80° = 180°, so...
c = 180° − 130° (50° + 80° = 130°)
c = 50°

---

8 Calculate the size of the missing angles.

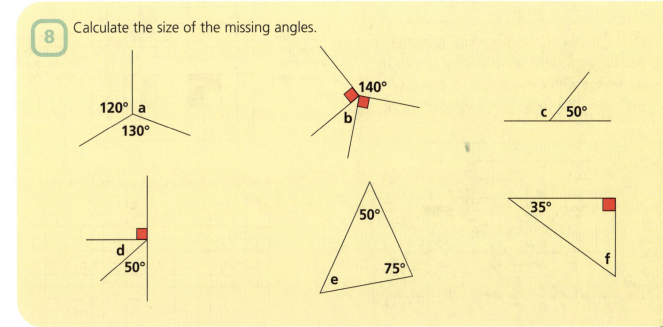

120° a
130°

140°
b

c 50°

d
50°

50°
e 75°

35°
f

Shape, Space and Measures

Line Symmetry

If we **fold** this page down its middle, **one half** goes **exactly on top** of the **other half**.

The page is folded along a **line of symmetry**. It also has another **line of symmetry** across its middle. We say the shape has **two lines of symmetry**.

Lines of symmetry can be found by **folding** the shape or using a **mirror**. If a **mirror** is placed on a **line of symmetry**, the shape looks just the same as without the mirror. This is sometimes called a **mirror line**.

A **line of symmetry** is usually shown by a **dotted line**. Line symmetry is also called **reflective symmetry**.

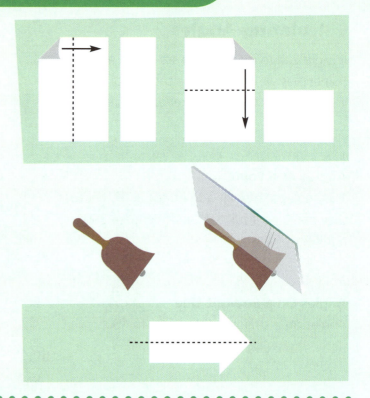

Reflection

A shape can be **reflected** in a **mirror line**. Using a **mirror** can be very helpful.

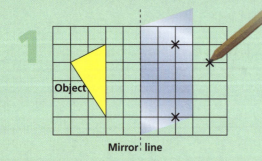

Place a mirror on the mirror line. Note the position of the reflection. Mark the corners of the **image** with a pencil. Keep checking with the mirror that they are in the correct place.

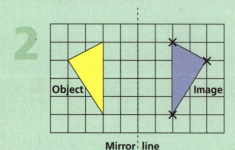

Join the corners. Double check with your mirror.

- The shape you start with is called the **object**. The shape you draw is called the **image**.
- The reflection of a point is the **same distance** from the mirror line, measured at **right angles** to the line.

Sometimes you are asked to reflect in two mirror lines.

Reflect the shape in one of the mirror lines.

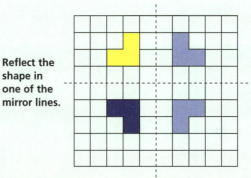

Then reflect both shapes in the second mirror line.

9 Reflect each shape in the mirror lines.

a)
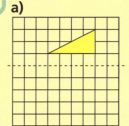

b)
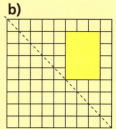

38

Translation

A **translation slides** a shape around. The shape does not turn or flip over. A **translation** is a combination of a **slide** to the **right** or **left**, and/or a **slide up** or **down**.

In a **translation** of **6 places right** and **3 places down**, each point of the object moves **6 places right** and **3 places down**. All you have to do is move each **corner**, marking its new position. Then join the corners together.

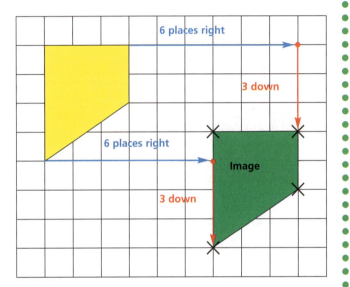

---

10 Copy this shape onto squared paper and translate it 4 places left and 2 places up.

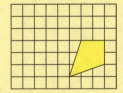

11 Copy this shape and the centre of rotation. Rotate it ¼ turn anti-clockwise.

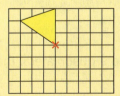

Rotation

A shape **rotates** about a **point** called the **centre of rotation**, by an amount of **turn**, in either a ⟩ **clockwise** or ⟨ **anti-clockwise** direction. **Tracing paper** makes doing **rotations** much easier.

For a rotation of a ¼ turn in a clockwise direction.

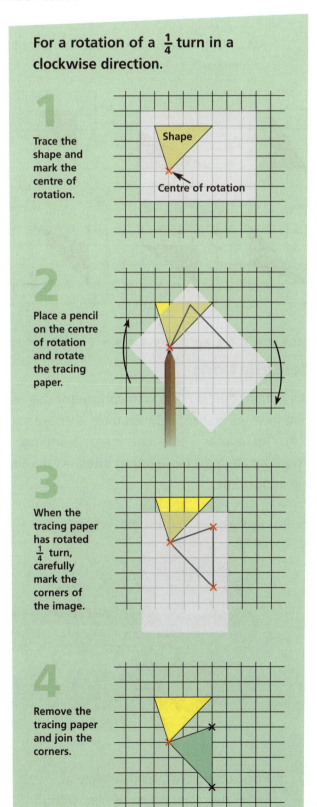

1 Trace the shape and mark the centre of rotation.

2 Place a pencil on the centre of rotation and rotate the tracing paper.

3 When the tracing paper has rotated ¼ turn, carefully mark the corners of the image.

4 Remove the tracing paper and join the corners.

Shape, Space and Measures

Congruent Shapes

Two shapes are **congruent** if they are exactly the same **size** and **shape**. If one of the shapes could be cut out and placed on top of the other shape so that it covers it exactly, then the two shapes are **congruent**.

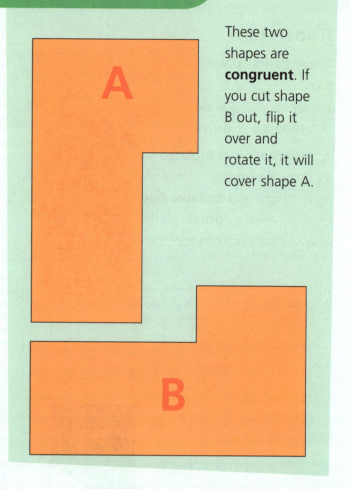

These two shapes are **congruent**. If you cut shape B out, flip it over and rotate it, it will cover shape A.

12 Which of the shapes below are congruent with shape A?

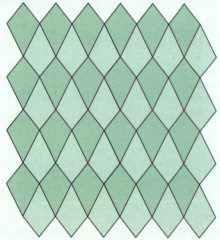

Tessellations

If a pattern can be made with **congruent** shapes, so that there are no gaps between them, then we say the shape **tessellates**. This is sometimes called **tiling**. This is a pattern of **tessellating kites**. All the kites are **congruent**.

These **octagons** are **congruent**, and they form a pattern, but there are gaps between them, so they **do not tessellate**.

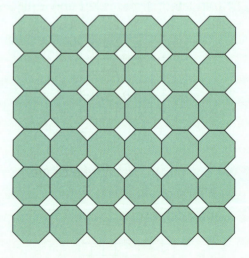

13 Philip claims that, 'all quadrilaterals tessellate'. Can you prove him wrong?

See if you can find a quadrilateral that will not tessellate.

Making 3-D Models

Next time you open a cereal packet, have a look at how the box is made. It is probably made out of just **one piece** of cardboard glued together. If you opened it up carefully it would look similar to this:

The grey parts are **flaps** used to glue the box together. The rest is called the **net** of the box.

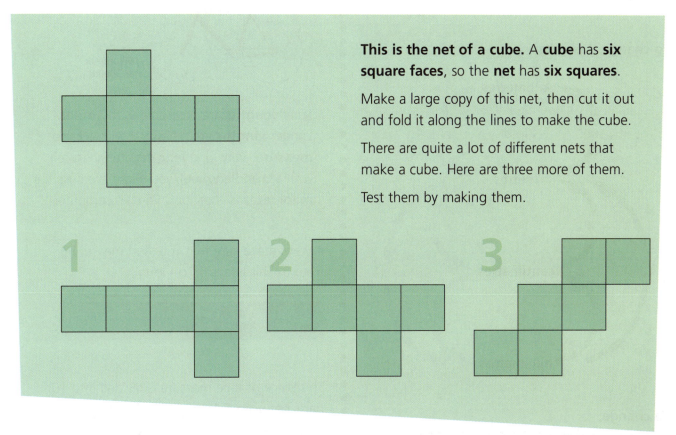

This is the net of a cube. A cube has **six square faces**, so the **net** has **six squares**.

Make a large copy of this net, then cut it out and fold it along the lines to make the cube.

There are quite a lot of different nets that make a cube. Here are three more of them.

Test them by making them.

1 2 3

The net of this triangular prism is shown below.
These two **edges** join together so they must be exactly the
same length.

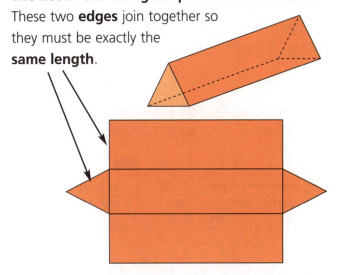

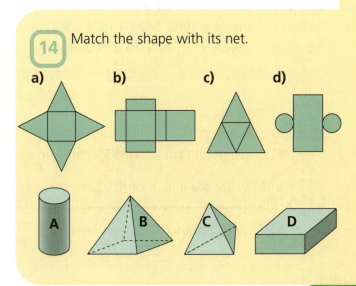

14 Match the shape with its net.

a) b) c) d)

A B C D

Shape, Space and Measures

Length

Length is measured in millimetres (mm), centimetres (cm), metres (m) and kilometres (km).

You need to know these:

1000mm = 1m
10mm = 1cm
100cm = 1m
1000m = 1km

We sometimes need to change from one unit to another.

To change the units:

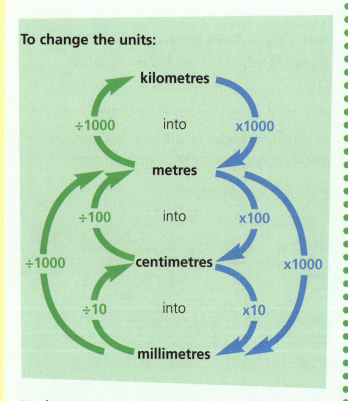

To change:

3.6m into cm we x 100: **3.6 x 100 = 360cm**
63mm into cm we ÷ 10: **63 ÷ 10 = 6.3cm**
5426m into km we ÷ 1000: **5426 ÷ 1000 = 5.426km**
38cm into mm we x 10: **38 x 10 = 380mm**

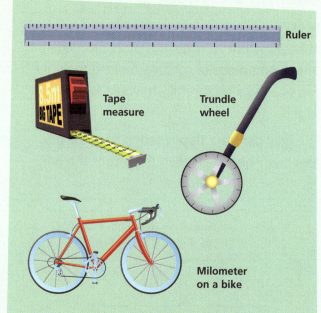

Small **lengths** are measured with a **ruler**. Longer **lengths** are measured with a **tape measure**. Very long **lengths** are measured with a **trundle wheel**, you might even use the **milometer** in a car or on a bike computer!

Always make sure that you start measuring from 0. This line is 5.7cm long.

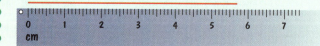

This piece of tape measure is divided into 10 parts between 6.1 and 6.2m. This marker flag is at 6.16m.

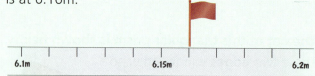

15 Change the following:
a) 3.2km into m
b) 4.3m into cm
c) 2.65m into mm
d) 11cm into mm
e) 64.2mm into cm
f) 3500mm into m
g) 70cm into m
h) 23 000m into km

16 a) Measure the length of this line.

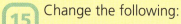

b) At what distance is this marker flag?

Mass

Mass is a measure of how **heavy** something is. **Mass** is measured in grams (g), kilograms (kg) and tonnes (t).

You need to know these:

1000g = 1kg
1000kg = 1t

To change the units:

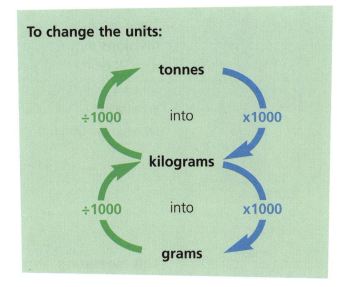

To change:

2.5t into kg we x 1000
2.5 x 1000 = 2500kg

0.8kg into g we x 1000
0.8 x 1000 = 800g

1900kg into t we ÷ 1000
1900 ÷ 1000 = 1.9t

640g into kg we ÷ 1000
640 ÷ 1000 = 0.64kg

Mass can be measured using a **spring balance** or **scales**.

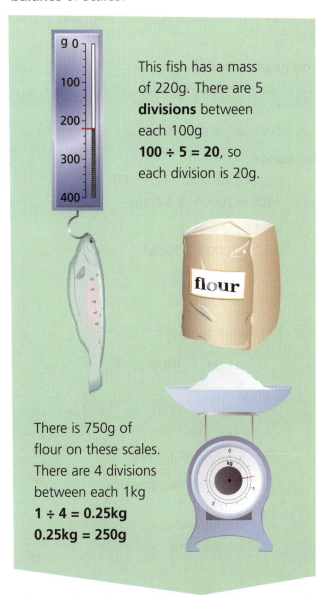

This fish has a mass of 220g. There are 5 **divisions** between each 100g
100 ÷ 5 = 20, so each division is 20g.

There is 750g of flour on these scales. There are 4 divisions between each 1kg
1 ÷ 4 = 0.25kg
0.25kg = 250g

---

17 Change the following:

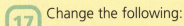

a) 4.35t into kg   **b)** 1.2kg into g   **c)** 31 300kg into t   **d)** 260g into kg

18 What is the reading on these scales?

a)    **b)**    **c)**    **d)**    **e)**   **f)**

Shape, Space and Measures

Capacity

Capacity is a measure of the amount of **space inside** something. **Capacity** is measured in millilitres (ml), centimetres cubed (cm³) and litres (l).

You need to know these:

$1ml = 1cm^3$
$1000ml = 1litre$
$1000cm^3 = 1litre$

To change:

3400ml into litres we ÷ 1000
3400 ÷ 1000 = 3.4 litres

0.63 litres into cm³ we x 1000
0.63 x 1000 = 630cm³

To change the units:

litres

÷1000   into   x1000

millilitres
=
cubic centimetres

(Millilitres and cubic centimetres are the same. 3ml = 3cm³).

Capacity can be measured in a **measuring cylinder** or **jug**.

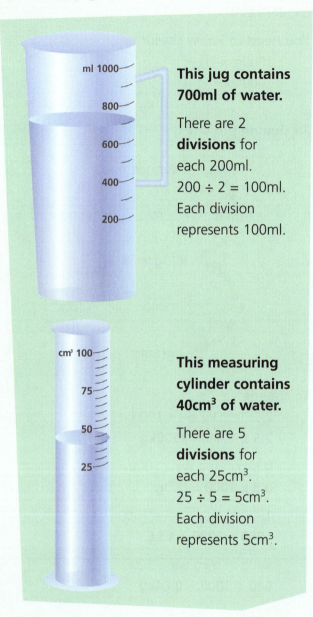

This jug contains 700ml of water.

There are 2 **divisions** for each 200ml.
200 ÷ 2 = 100ml.
Each division represents 100ml.

This measuring cylinder contains 40cm³ of water.

There are 5 **divisions** for each 25cm³.
25 ÷ 5 = 5cm³.
Each division represents 5cm³.

---

19 Change the following:
a) 2.3 litres into ml
b) 14.25 litres into cm³
c) 850ml into litres
d) 115cm³ into litres
e) 7.5 litres into ml
f) 9.25 litres into cm³
g) 625ml into litres
h) 95cm³ into litres
i) 165cm³ into litres

20 How much water is in each of the containers?

a)

b)

c)

Shape, Space and Measures

Time

Time is measured in seconds (s), minutes (min), hours (hrs), days, weeks, months and years.

You need to know these:

60 seconds	= 1 minute
60 minutes	= 1 hour
24 hours	= 1 day
7 days	= 1 week
365 days	= 1 year (or 366 in a leap year)
10 years	= 1 decade
100 years	= 1 century
1000 years	= 1 millennium

'30 days have September, April, June and November. All the rest have 31, excepting February alone, which has 28 days clear, and 29 in each leap year'.

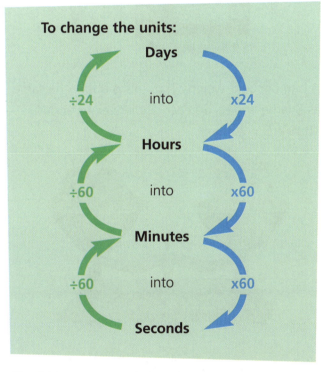

To change the units:

Days

÷24   into   x24

Hours

÷60   into   x60

Minutes

÷60   into   x60

Seconds

To change:

$2\frac{1}{2}$ minutes into seconds we x 60

$2\frac{1}{2}$ x 60 = 150 seconds

400 minutes into hours we ÷ 60

400 ÷ 60 = 6 remainder 40

So 400 minutes = 6 hours 40 minutes.

340 hours into days we ÷ 24

340 ÷ 24 = 14 remainder 4

So 340 hours = 14 days 4 hours.

Decimals are only used with seconds.

Finding the Difference in Time

If a film starts at 5.40pm and finishes at 7.30pm, how long it has lasted is found most easily by **adding on**.

From: 5.40 until 6.00 is 20 minutes.
      6.00 until 7.00 is 1 hour.
      7.00 until 7.30 is 30 minutes.

Total time = 20 minutes + 1 hour + 30 minutes
           = 1 hour 50 minutes.

The 24 Hour Clock

A clock usually has 12 hours on it. The 12 hours before midday are am and after midday they are pm. In **24 hour clock** time, am or pm are not needed.

3.00pm = 15.00   6.30am = 06.30   12.17am = 00.17

21 Change the following:
  a) 300 seconds into minutes.
  b) 4 days into hours.
  c) 5 hours into minutes.
  d) 250 minutes into hours.

22 How long is it from:
  a) 6.30am to 9.15am?
  b) 11.15am to 2.30pm?
  c) 08.20 to 14.10?

Shape, Space and Measures

Imperial Units

Imperial units used to be used throughout the old British Empire. They are still used quite a lot so we need to know roughly what measurements in imperial units are in metric units.

Length

2.5cm ≈ 1 inch.
30cm ≈ 1 foot. (≈ means 'is roughly')
'1m is a bit bigger than 1 yard'.

So 5m is a bit more than 5 yards, and 3 inches is roughly 3 x 2.5 = 7.5cm.

Mass

'2.2 pounds of jam weighs about a kilogram' or 1kg is a bit **more** than 2 pounds. (1 pound is written 1lb)

1lb + 1lb + 0.2lb = 1kg

So 5kg is a bit more than 10 pounds.

Capacity

'A litre of water is a pint and three quarters' or 1 litre is a bit **less** than 2 pints.

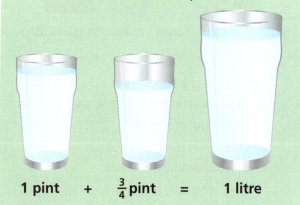

1 pint + ¾ pint = 1 litre

So 3 litres is a bit less than 6 pints, and 8 pints is a bit more than 4 litres.

Estimating Measures

When you are trying to **estimate** a measure, compare the thing you are estimating with something you know the size of.

A double decker bus is about $2\frac{1}{2}$ times the height of an adult. An adult is about 1.8m high so the bus is about 4.5m high.

A bag of sugar weighs 1kg, this is about the same as 5 large apples. So each apple weighs about 1000 ÷ 5 = 200g.

23
a) 15 pounds = ? kg   f) 20cm = ? inch
b) 6 inches = ? cm   g) 20 pints = ? litres
c) 5 litres = ? pints   h) 20 inches = ? cm
d) 5kg = ? pounds   i) 3 feet = ? cm
e) 75cm = ? feet   j) 100 litres = ? pints

24
a) Estimate the height of a house.
b) If 1 litre of water weighs 1kg, what does 8 pints of water weigh?
c) Estimate the height of your classroom in metres and yards.

Perimeter

Perimeter is the **distance** all the way around the outside. If you walk all the way around the outside of your school grounds, you will walk the **perimeter** of the grounds.

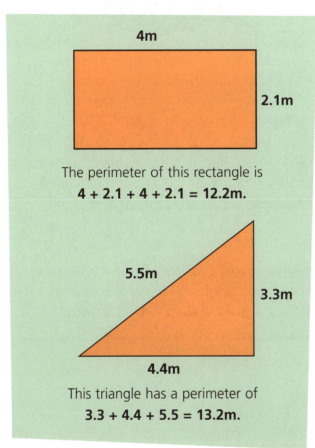

The perimeter of this rectangle is
4 + 2.1 + 4 + 2.1 = 12.2m.

This triangle has a perimeter of
3.3 + 4.4 + 5.5 = 13.2m.

Because the opposite sides of a rectangle are the same length, you will always have two pairs of equal sides. So you could find the perimeter of the rectangle above by adding the two given sides together and then doubling your answer.

$$4 + 2.1 = 6.1m$$
$$6.1 \times 2 = 12.2m$$

If you are not given all the lengths, you may be able to calculate the missing ones.

This side must be **4 – 2 = 2cm**
This side must be **7 – 3 = 4cm**

This shape has a perimeter of
7 + 4 + 3 + 2 + 4 + 2 = 22cm

If the shape is drawn accurately you can use a ruler to measure the length of the sides.

25 Find the perimeter of these shapes.
Only d) is drawn accurately.

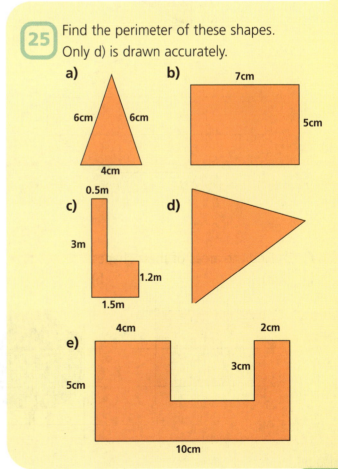

Shape, Space and Measures

Area

The **area** of a shape is a measure of how much of a surface it covers. It is usually measured in square millimetres (mm²), square centimetres (cm²) or square metres (m²).

The **area** of a shape can be found by counting how many centimetre squares or metre squares it covers.

If the shape does not cover some of the squares **exactly**, we can approximate the **area**. Squares which are at least half covered are counted as 1 square. Squares that are less than half covered are ignored.

This rectangle covers 8 centimetre squares. So it has an area of 8cm².

This leaf is approximately 10cm².

Ignore this square as it is less than half covered

Ignore this square as it is less than half covered

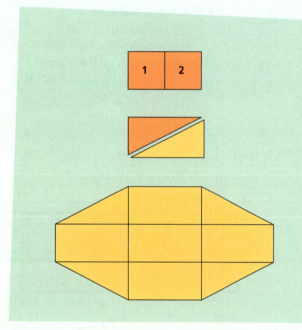

This rectangle has an area of **2cm²**.

It can be cut in **half** to give two triangles. Each triangle will have **half** the area of the rectangle. Each triangle will have an area of **1cm²**.

This shape is made up from 5 of the rectangles and 4 of the triangles, so it has an area of **2 + 2 + 2 + 2 + 2 + 1 + 1 + 1 + 1 = 14cm²**.

26 Find the areas of these shapes.

a)   b)   c)

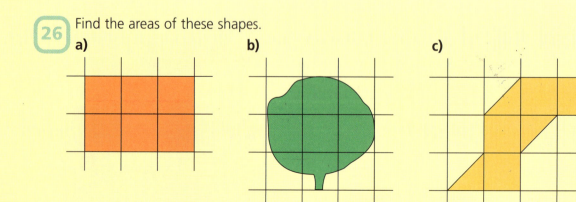

Shape, Space and Measures

More Area

We could find the area of this page by covering it in centimetre squares and then counting them – but there is a quicker way.

A rectangle that is 5cm across and 3cm down, has 5 lots of 3 squares inside it. So the area is $5 \times 3 = 15cm^2$.

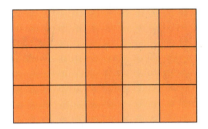

It doesn't matter which side is the length and which is the width, but they must have the same units.
- If they are in mm, the area is in mm^2.
- If they are in cm, the area is in cm^2.
- If they are in m, the area is in m^2.

This method works for any rectangle and can be written as a formula.

Area = Length x Width

This page is 29.7cm long and 21cm wide so it has an area of $29.7 \times 21 = 623.7cm^2$

One Interesting Point

Drawing a diagonal across a rectangle makes two right angled triangles. The area of each triangle is half of the area of the rectangle. So we can calculate the area of a right angled triangle by using the formula for a rectangle and then halving the answer.

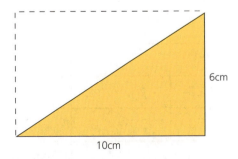

Area of rectangle = 10 x 6 = 60cm²
Area of triangle = 60 ÷ 2 = 30cm²

The formula for the area of a rectangle can be used to help calculate the area of shapes that are made up of two or more rectangles.
- Split the shape into rectangles.
- Find the length and width of each rectangle.
- Calculate the area of each rectangle.
- Add these together to get the total area of the shape.

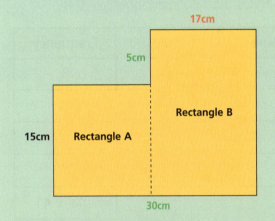

Rectangle A is 15cm long and $30 - 17 = 13$cm wide
Rectangle B is $15 + 5 = 20$cm long and 17cm wide
Area of rectangle A = $15 \times 13 = 195cm^2$
Area of rectangle B = $20 \times 17 = 340cm^2$

Total area = 195 + 340 = 535cm²

27 Calculate the areas of these shapes.

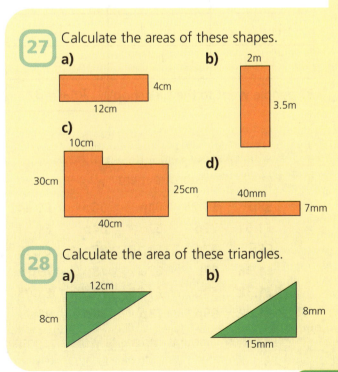

a) 12cm, 4cm
b) 2m, 3.5m
c) 10cm, 30cm, 40cm, 25cm
d) 40mm, 7mm

28 Calculate the area of these triangles.
a) 12cm, 8cm
b) 8mm, 15mm

Handling Data

Collecting Data

Data can be collected quickly and accurately using a **tally chart**. Michael, Kiera, Daniel and Sophie are seeing how many times they can run around the school hall in 5 minutes. Pravesh keeps a record of each lap completed. Every time someone runs past he puts a **tally mark** against their name (the **fifth** tally is diagonal). **The frequency column is the total of the tallies.** At the end of the 5 minutes, his tally chart looks like this:

Name	Tally	Frequency
Michael	‖‖ ‖‖ ‖‖	8
Kiera	‖‖‖ ‖‖‖ ‖‖‖‖	14
Daniel	‖‖‖ ‖‖‖ ‖‖	12
Sophie	‖‖‖ ‖‖	7
	Total = **41**

Lucy is recording how much people spend at the school tuck shop. Because people spend lots of different amounts, she puts the amounts into **groups**.

Amount spent	Tally	Frequency
1–20p	‖‖‖ ‖	6
21–40p	‖‖‖ ‖‖‖ ‖‖‖ ‖	16
41–60p	‖‖‖ ‖‖‖ ‖‖	12
61–80p	‖‖‖	3
37 people went to the tuck shop	Total = **37**

---

1 A shopkeeper kept a record of how much 30 customers spent.

58p	£1.25	84p	96p	£1.44
£1.01	72p	52p	64p	£1.31
88p	97p	£1.10	93p	£1.15
£1.36	87p	67p	78p	79p
£1.32	59p	£1.25	£1.26	£1.08
£1.02	95p	73p	86p	91p

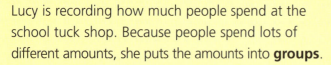

Put these amounts into the tally chart opposite.

Amount spent	Tally	Frequency
51p–75p		
76p–£1.00		
£1.01–£1.25		
£1.26–£1.50		
		Total =

Bar Charts

Pravesh decided to display the data he collected in his tally chart using a **bar chart**. The **bars** could be **vertical** or **horizontal**. Sometimes lines are drawn instead of bars. This is called a **bar line chart**.

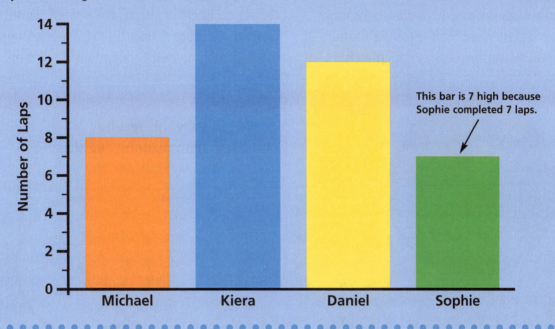

This bar is 7 high because Sophie completed 7 laps.

Pictograms

Lucy decided to display the data she had collected at the tuck shop in a **pictogram**. The symbols must all start in a line. All the symbols must be the **same size** and **equally spaced**. Use a symbol that is relevant to the data.

Key: 🥔 = 2 customers

Amount spent	Number of people spending that amount
1–20p	🥔 🥔 🥔
21–40p	🥔 🥔 🥔 🥔 🥔 🥔 🥔 🥔
41–60p	🥔 🥔 🥔 🥔 🥔 🥔
61–80p	🥔 🥔 ← This $\frac{1}{2}$ symbol represents 1 customer.

2

a) Finish off this bar chart for the data the shopkeeper collected.

b) Draw a pictogram for the data Pravesh collected on laps of the school hall.

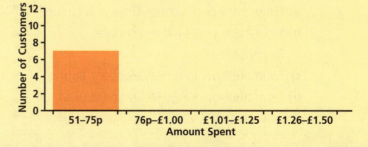

Handling Data

Pie Charts

Pie charts are a good way of showing how something is divided up. For instance, how the opinion of your class is divided. Andrew asked the 32 people in his class what their favourite flavours of crisp were. His results are shown in this **pie chart**.

$\frac{3}{8}$ of the pie chart is Salt & Vinegar.
So $\frac{3}{8}$ of the 32 pupils chose Salt & Vinegar.
$\frac{3}{8}$ **of 32 = 12 pupils**.

Hayley drew a pie chart of how she spent her day. She spent about $\frac{1}{3}$ of her day sleeping. $\frac{1}{3}$ **of 24 = 8** so she spent about **8 hours sleeping**.

We can only estimate, unless we know the exact size of the angles.

Sorting Diagrams

Diagrams are used to make information clearer. **Sorting diagrams** can be used to show how certain numbers or shapes are related. James is looking at numbers from 1 – 10. He is sorting them into prime numbers and even numbers.

He can show his result…

… in a venn diagram like this.

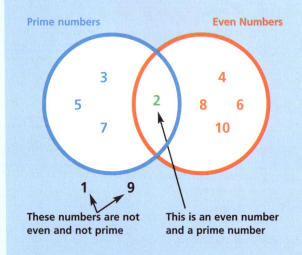

Another useful sorting diagram…

…is a carroll diagram.

	Prime	Not Prime
Even	2	8 4 6 10
Not Even	5 7 3	1 9

---

 a) How many pupils chose Cheese & Onion?
b) How many pupils did not choose Ready Salted?
c) Estimate how long Hayley spent eating.
d) Estimate how long Hayley spent playing or watching T.V.

 a) Put these numbers on the Venn diagram below: 3, 4, 6, 15, 20
b) Sort the same numbers using a Carroll diagram.

Even numbers Multiples of 3

Line Graphs

Line graphs can be used to show what is happening over a period of time.

This graph shows Peter's progress in the Great 10km Run. The distance that he had run was recorded at 10 minute intervals. The crosses on the graph show these distances.

We can tell from the graph that Peter had run $1\frac{1}{2}$ km after 10 minutes because the cross is exactly halfway between the 1km and 2km divisions.

On this graph, the line inbetween the crosses shows the approximate distances that Peter had run at times inbetween the 10 minute intervals.

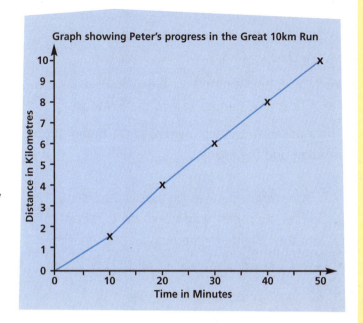

Graph showing Peter's progress in the Great 10km Run

5 Liam records his weight every month for one year. The results are as follows. Draw a line graph to show his weight.

Month	JAN	FEB	MAR	APR	MAY	JUN	JUL	AUG	SEPT	OCT	NOV	DEC
Liam's weight (kg)	60	61	61	63	64	63	63	61	59	58	58	57

Types of Data

Data that can only have certain values is called discrete data.

The number of goals scored in a football match goes up in whole numbers. You cannot score 1.9 goals. The shoes in a shoe shop go up in half sizes. You cannot buy size 10.2 shoes. You have to buy either size 10 or size $10\frac{1}{2}$. In other words, discrete data goes up in jumps. Other examples of discrete data are the number of oranges in a box, or the number of hairs on your head.

Data that can have any value and is recorded using measuring instruments is called continuous data.

For example, the mass of an apple could be 103.9g or 103.86g. The only limit on the number of decimal places is the accuracy of the weighing scales. Other examples of continuous data are heights of trees or amount of juice in a lemon.

Usually, if the data is counted it is discrete and if the data is measured it is continuous.

6 Say whether this data is discrete or continuous.
a) Number of potatoes in a sack.

b) Mass of a sack of potatoes.
c) Amount of pocket money a child gets.

Handling Data

Averages

In its last 10 matches, the school football team scored: 1, 2, 5, 0, 3, 7, 4, 4, 2, 4 goals.

Penny is writing a report for the West Park School Newsletter. She decides to find the **average**.

There are three types of **average**: the **mean**, the **median** and the **mode**.

– **The mean** is the average used most often. To find the **mean**, **add up** all the numbers and then **divide** by the number of numbers.

   1 + 2 + 5 + 0 + 3 + 7 + 4 + 4 + 2 + 4 = 32

   32 goals were scored altogether in 10 matches. The **mean is 32 ÷ 10 = 3.2 goals.**

– **The median** is found by placing all the numbers in order, from smallest to largest. The **median** is the middle number. If there are two numbers in the middle, the **median** is halfway between these two.

   Putting the number of goals scored in order we get: **0, 1, 2, 2, 3, 4, 4, 4, 5, 7**

   The middle two numbers are **3** and **4**. Halfway between **3** and **4** is **3.5**. The **median** is **3.5**.

– **The mode** is the number that occurs the most often.

   4 goals were scored in 3 of the matches, 4 is the most common score. So the **mode** is **4**.

The WPS Newsletter
SPRING TERM 2007
Extra Funding for the New Sixth Form Common Room

Pupils Fight Tuck Shop Closure

FOOTBALL LEAGUE VICTORY IN SIGHT

A l... happen in 45 minutes.

---

7 The temperature in °C at 12 noon each day over two weeks in July was: 22, 23, 25, 27, 28, 24, 21, 20, 22, 22, 21, 23, 24, 26. Find:
  a) The mean.
  b) The median.
  c) The mode.
  d) The range of these temperatures.

The Range

The **range** of a set of numbers tells us how **spread out** those numbers are.

The range = Biggest Number – Smallest Number

The **range** for goals scored in the football matches is **7 – 0 = 7.**

Probability

Probability is a measure of **how likely** something is to happen. We can use words to describe the **probability** of an event happening. **Probability** goes from **impossible** to **certain**. Words like 'evens' means halfway between **certain** and **impossible**. There are lots of words you could use to describe the probability of something happening. This can be shown on a **probability scale**. You may not agree with the position of every word on the probability scale.

Predicting Outcomes

A die has six sides, each with a different number from 1 to 6 on it. Everytime you roll the die, each number has an equal 'one in six' chance of being thrown. For example, the chance of throwing a 3 is 'one in six' or $\frac{1}{6}$ each time. However, calculating the probability of an outcome is not always this straightforward.

Here are two spinners. The number 5 appears more times on spinner B, but this does not mean that it is more likely to land on a 5 than spinner A. You need to look at the fraction of the spinner taken up by the 5s. There is a 'three in eight' or $\frac{3}{8}$ chance of landing on a 5 with spinner B. There is a 'one in two' or $\frac{1}{2}$ chance of landing on a 5 with spinner A. In other words, there is a greater chance with spinner A.

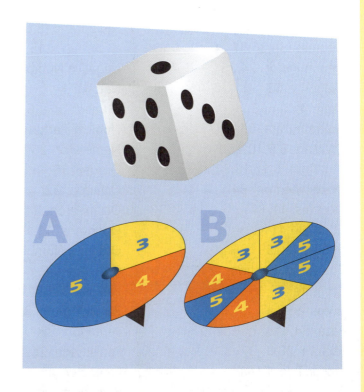

8 John says there is an evens chance of getting a 6 using these three spinners. Is he correct? Explain your answers.

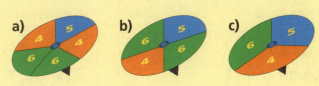

a)   b)   c)

Index

Acute 35
Adding 10,11,12,19
Algebra 23
Angle 33,35,36,37
Area 48,49
Average 54
Axis 31,51,53
Bar Chart 51
Bisect 33
Capacity 44,46
Carroll Diagram 52
Certainty 55
Co-ordinates 31
Concave 32
Convex 32
Congruent 40
Continuous Data 53
Corner 34
Cube 34,41
Cuboid 34
Cylinder 34
Data 50,53
Decimal Point 4,9,12
Decimal Fraction 4,18
Decimals 6,9,12,17,18,26
Degrees 35,36,37
Denominator 24,25
Diagonal 33
Digit 4, 5, 6, 8
Discrete Data 53
Dividing 8,9,10,13,14,
        16,17,18,24,25
Dodecahedron 34
Doubles 11,14
Edge 34,41
Equilateral 33
Equivalent Fractions 24,28
Estimate 30,46
Evens 55
Face 34,41
Factors 20
Factor Tree 21
Figures 5
Formulas 23
Fractions 24,25,26,27
Frequency 50
Greater Than 7

Grouping 16
Halves 14
Hemisphere 34
Hexagon 32,34
Image 38
Imperial Units 46
Impossibility 55
Improper Fraction 25
Intersect 33
Isosceles 33
Kite 33
Length 42,46
Less Than 7
Line Graph 53
Line Symmetry 38
Long Multiplication 15,17
Lowest Common Multiple 20
Mass 43,46
Mean 54
Median 54
Mirror Line 38
Mixed Number 25
Mode 54
Multiples 20
Multiplying 8,9,10,13,14,
        15,17,24,25
Negative Numbers 7,19,31
Net 41
Number Line 6,7,11,19,25,26
Number Patterns 22
Numerator 25
Obtuse 35
Octagon 32
Octahedron 34
Opposites 11,17
Ordering Numbers 6
Outcome 55
Parallel 32,33
Parallelogram 33
Pentagon 32
Percentage 26,27,28
Perimeter 47
Perpendicular 34
Pictogram 51
Pie Chart 52
Place Value 4, 5
Polygon 32,33,34

Polyhedron 34
Prime Factors 21
Prime Numbers 21
Prism 34,41
Probability 55
Proportion 28
Protractor 36
Pyramid 34
Quadrilateral 32,33
Range 54
Ratio 28
Rectangle 33,49
Reflection 38
Reflex Angle 35
Regular Polygon 32
Remainder 18
Rhombus 33
Right Angle 33,34,35,49
Rotation 35,39
Rounding 30
Rule 22,23
Scalene 33
Shapes 32,33,34
Simplifying Fractions 25
Solid 34
Solving Problems 29
Sphere 34
Square 33
Square Numbers 21
Subtracting 10,11,12,19
Symmetry 38
Tally Chart 50
Temperature 7,19
Term 22
Tessellate 40
Tetrahedron 34
Three-dimensions 34,41
Time 45
Times tables 13
Translation 39
Trapezium 33
Triangle 32,33
Venn Diagram 52
Vertex 34
Zero 4